Lucifer

Devil in the Gateway

Mike Carey
Writer

Scott Hampton
Chris Weston
James Hodgkins
Warren Pleece
Dean Ormston
Artists

Daniel Vozzo
Colorist

Todd Klein
Ellie de Ville
Letterers

Neil Gaiman
Consultant

Based on characters created by Neil Gaiman,
Sam Kieth and Mike Dringenberg

LUCIFER: DEVIL IN THE GATEWAY

Published by DC Comics. Cover, foreword and compilation
copyright © 2001 DC Comics. All Rights Reserved.

Originally published in single magazine form as
THE SANDMAN PRESENTS: LUCIFER 1-3 and
LUCIFER 1-4. Copyright © 1999, 2000 DC Comics.
All Rights Reserved.

DC Comics, 1700 Broadway, New York, NY 10019
A Warner Bros. Entertainment Company
Printed in Canada. Third Printing.
ISBN: 1-56389-733-4

Collection cover composited from covers for LUCIFER 2 and 4,
originally painted by Duncan Fegredo

THE LIGHT BRINGER

Writing Lucifer was never hard, not in the way that some other writing was hard. His stories, and his alone, would turn up in my head with beginnings, and middles, and ends. Of all the hundreds of characters in THE SANDMAN, he, above all, had his own agenda from the moment he first came on stage.

I took him, or went with him, on his journey from ruler of Hell in THE SANDMAN #4 (there was a nominal triumvirate in charge at the time, imposed by DC's head office, but you always knew which member of the triumvirate called the shots); to his resignation in the "Season of Mists" story — during the course of which he closed Hell, quit, kissed Mazikeen goodbye, and had his wings cut off; and from there to a nightclub called Lux, where he played cocktail piano and watched everyone else's problems with amused disdain.

He might only have been a supporting character in the SANDMAN story, but there was no doubt in my mind that he was a star.

Lucifer needed his own comic. It seemed obvious, at least to me. He was arrogant, funny, manipulative, cold, brilliant, powerful, and the former Lord of Hell, who resigned because he was done. Heaven wouldn't trust him, Hell would hate him, but anyone who needed a dirty job done would approach Lucifer to do it. (That would have been my approach, anyway.)

Sometime in 1991 I had a meeting in a hotel room with a writer who wanted to write something for VERTIGO. He asked me if there was any character I'd suggest pitching to the powers that be at VERTIGO as a spinoff series.

"Lucifer," I said.

He looked doubtful. I tried to reassure him by explaining what kind of comic it could be, invoking everything from the Kabala to Hannibal Heyes and Kid Curry in *Alias Smith and Jones* ("I sure wish the governor would let a few more people in on our secret!"), and at the end of our conversation he looked no less doubtful than he had looked at the start.

"Anybody else?" he said.

It was a question I slowly grew used to as the decade continued. "Who'd make a good spinoff character?"

"Lucifer," I'd say.

And, like the writer in the hotel room, they'd say, "Anyone else?" I think they were mostly worried that a comic starring the Devil (even a Devil who had got bored, and tired, and resigned) might lead somebody to burn down the DC offices. This was particularly true when they were located at 666 Fifth Avenue.

And anyway, to tell good Lucifer stories, we would need a good writer.

In this case, a writer named Mike Carey. Who got it, without needing it to be explained. Mike Carey's Lucifer is even more manipulative, charming and dangerous than I could have hoped. The supporting cast are real people, living and dead, in a real world. Carey's stories are elegantly told, solidly written (for my money, he's easily one of the half-dozen best writers of mainstream comics, and climbing), and they are good comics. Which, like the people in them, are going somewhere.

His collaborators are doing an excellent job of picturing Mike's world.

I still expect the success of Lucifer to prompt someone with more convictions than sense to attempt to burn down the DC offices. Until they do, I shall keep reading.

— *Neil Gaiman*
The Ice Hotel, Québec
February 2001

The Morningstar Option

Mike Carey
Writer

Scott Hampton
Artist

Todd Klein
Letterer

Jennifer Lee
Assistant Editor

Alisa Kwitney
Editor

Neil Gaiman
Consultant

AS HOC OPUS HIC

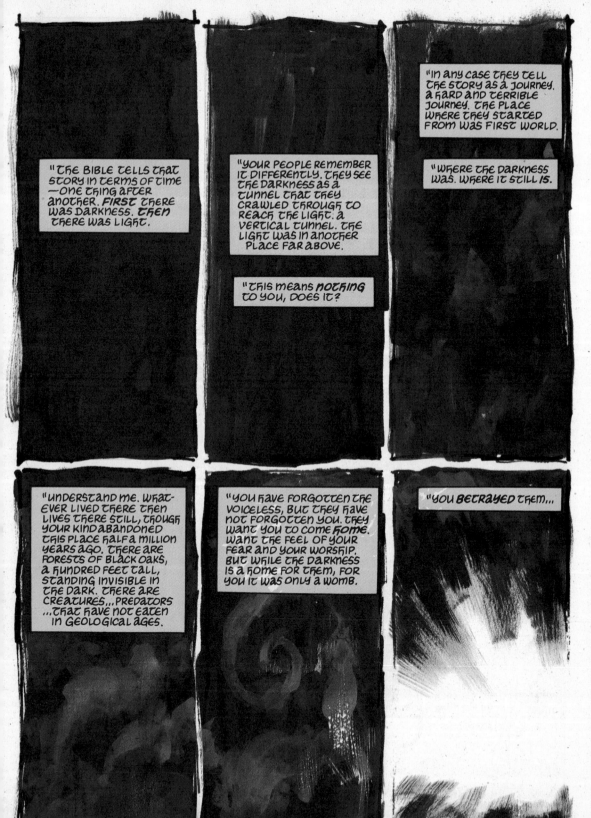

"THE BIBLE TELLS THAT STORY IN TERMS OF TIME —ONE THING AFTER ANOTHER. FIRST THERE WAS DARKNESS. THEN THERE WAS LIGHT.

"YOUR PEOPLE REMEMBER IT DIFFERENTLY. THEY SEE THE DARKNESS AS A TUNNEL THAT THEY CRAWLED THROUGH TO REACH THE LIGHT. A VERTICAL TUNNEL. THE LIGHT WAS IN ANOTHER PLACE FAR ABOVE.

"THIS MEANS NOTHING TO YOU, DOES IT?

"IN ANY CASE THEY TELL THE STORY AS A JOURNEY. A HARD AND TERRIBLE JOURNEY. THE PLACE WHERE THEY STARTED FROM WAS FIRST WORLD.

"WHERE THE DARKNESS WAS. WHERE IT STILL IS.

"UNDERSTAND ME. WHATEVER LIVED THERE THEN LIVES THERE STILL, THOUGH YOUR KIND ABANDONED THIS PLACE HALF A MILLION YEARS AGO. THERE ARE FORESTS OF BLACK OAKS, A HUNDRED FEET TALL, STANDING INVISIBLE IN THE DARK. THERE ARE CREATURES...PREDATORS ...THAT HAVE NOT EATEN IN GEOLOGICAL AGES.

"YOU HAVE FORGOTTEN THE VOICELESS, BUT THEY HAVE NOT FORGOTTEN YOU. THEY WANT YOU TO COME HOME. WANT THE FEEL OF YOUR FEAR AND YOUR WORSHIP. BUT WHILE THE DARKNESS IS A HOME FOR THEM, FOR YOU IT WAS ONLY A WOMB.

"YOU BETRAYED THEM...

"...WHEN YOU WERE BORN INTO THE LIGHT."

NO ASYMMETRY, BUT THE PUPILLARY DILATION *IS* ON THE SLOW SIDE.

IT'S OKAY, PAUL, THE LIGHT WON'T HURT YOU.

SEE THE PICTURE? THE BOY'S PLAYING WITH A *TRUCK*, ISN'T HE? CAN YOU POINT TO THE *TRUCK*? TRY TO POINT TO THE *TRUCK*, PAUL.

AUL HAS A TRUCK

RY RIDES A

LET'S FEEL THOSE FINGERS. OH, GOOD GRIP, PAUL. NICE GRIP. HE'S LEFT-HANDED, ISN'T HE? LET'S TRY THE OTHER SIDE.

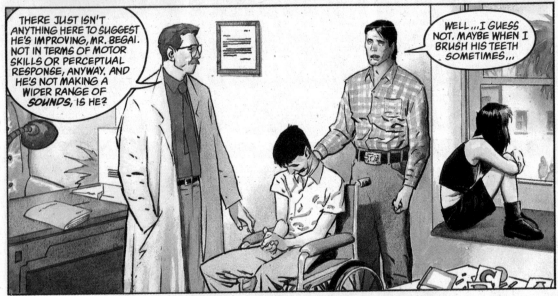

THERE JUST ISN'T ANYTHING HERE TO SUGGEST HE'S IMPROVING, MR. BEGAI. NOT IN TERMS OF MOTOR SKILLS OR PERCEPTUAL RESPONSE, ANYWAY. AND HE'S NOT MAKING A WIDER RANGE OF *SOUNDS*, IS HE?

WELL...I GUESS NOT. MAYBE WHEN I BRUSH HIS TEETH SOMETIMES...

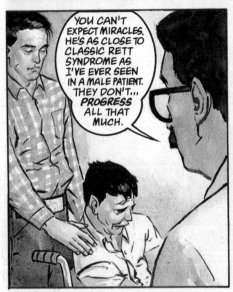

YOU CAN'T EXPECT MIRACLES. HE'S AS CLOSE TO CLASSIC RETT SYNDROME AS I'VE EVER SEEN IN A MALE PATIENT. THEY DON'T... *PROGRESS* ALL THAT MUCH.

I WAS THINKIN'... I DUNNO... THAT HE WAS *LOOKIN'* AT ME MORE. LIKE HE WANTED TO TALK TO ME, ALMOST. YOU THINK THAT COULD EVER...?

NO. PUT THAT OUT OF YOUR MIND.

YOU SAID THE FITS ARE ACTUALLY WORSE NOW. DOES THAT MEAN LONGER OR MORE INTENSE?

WELL, BOTH.

I CAN UP THE DOSAGE ON THE LAMOTRIGINE BUT TRY USING THE RECTAL VALIUM TOO, AS A PREVENTATIVE...

"HE'S YOUR BROTHER. YOU'D WANT TO BE THERE FOR YOUR BROTHER, WOULDN'T YOU RACHEL?"

"YEAH, DAD, FINE. IT'S JUST A SCHOOL DAY. I'LL JUST MISS IT. NO PROBLEM. MY TIME IS YOURS."

"...OBVIOUSLY."

HEY, DAD--THERE'S SOME WEIRD WOMAN HANGING 'ROUND YOUR CAR.

I TOLD YOU NOT TO PARK THERE.

SHE'S ACTING REAL CRAZY. SHE'S WAVING THIS FLOWER AROUND LIKE SHE'S DIRECTING TRAFFIC. AND I THINK SHE'S CRYING.

MY GOD, HE LOVES ME! HE REALLY LOVES ME! OH JESUS, SWEET JESUS!

LOOK! I FOUND THIS!

THAT'S NICE. TAKE CARE. TAKE CARE, NOW.

LOCAL MAN JERRY RUFINO SPRAYED HIS BOSS WITH SHAVING FOAM WHEN HE WON THE STATE LOTTERY YESTERDAY, BUT TWELVE HOURS LATER HE WAS ASKING FOR HIS OLD JOB BACK...

I DUNNO ABOUT USIN' MORE OF THAT LAMOTRIGINE STUFF. IT ALWAYS LEAVES 'IM DOPEY. WHAT D'YOU RECKON, RACH?

...BECAUSE A STAGGERING EIGHT HUNDRED PEOPLE PICKED THE WINNING NUMBERS, EACH COLLECTING LESS THAN THREE THOUSAND DOLLARS! DON'T GIVE UP YOUR DAY JOB, JER.

WELL IF IT'S A CHOICE BETWEEN DOPEY AND FRENZY, I KNOW WHICH DWARF I'D GO FOR.

WHAT'S THAT, FLOWER?

NOTHING, DAD.

YOU KNOW HE IS USING HIS VOICE MORE. I WONDER IF WE COULD GET 'IM SOME KIND OF SPEECH THERAPY?

I APPRECIATE YOU LOOKIN' AFTER 'IM TONIGHT, FLOWER. I KNOW YOU WANTED TO GO OUT, BUT I GOTTA MAKE UP THE TIME AT THE SHOP.

NO PROBLEM. ALL PART OF THE SERVICE.

TCH. COME ON, PAUL, MOST CHICKS WON'T EVEN LOOK AT A GUY WITH DROOL ON HIS CHIN.

"THEN AGAIN, MOM LOOKED AT DAD."

"SO I GUESS THERE'S HOPE FOR ALL OF US."

LOS ANGELES, CALIFORNIA.

I have said that I wish to see the proprietor.

YES SIR. MAY I REFRESH YOUR NUTS?

You may leave my nuts *exactly* as they are. Tell your employer that I will speak with him.

YOU CAN CLOSE UP UNTIL TONIGHT, BEATRICE.

NO I CAN'T. THERE'S THIS FREAKY GUY SITTING OUT ON TABLE SEVEN, ALL BY HIMSELF. HE'S BEEN ASKING AFTER YOU.

YES. I IMAGINE HE HAS.

LOCK THE DOOR ANYWAY.

MAZIKEEN, BRING US TWO GLASSES FROM MY SPECIAL BOTTLE-- THE ONE ON THE LEFT.

"WHOSE FEET MAY NOT TOUCH THE GROUND, NOR ANY FOULNESS STAIN THEIR GARMENTS, FOR THEY ARE OF THE SEVENTH SPHERE WHICH IS ABOVE CORRUPTION."

The devil can cite scripture for his purpose. Good day to you, Lucifer Morningstar.

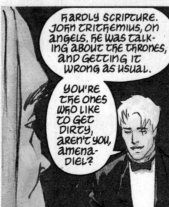

HARDLY SCRIPTURE. JOHN TRITHEMIUS, ON ANGELS. HE WAS TALKING ABOUT THE THRONES, AND GETTING IT WRONG AS USUAL.

YOU'RE THE ONES WHO LIKE TO GET DIRTY, AREN'T YOU, AMENA-DIEL?

There is no room for doubt or scruple in the service of the name. If you'd realized that you might still be of the host.

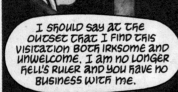

I SHOULD SAY AT THE OUTSET THAT I FIND THIS VISITATION BOTH IRKSOME AND UNWELCOME. I AM NO LONGER HELL'S RULER AND YOU HAVE NO BUSINESS WITH ME.

And how are you *finding* your retirement, Prince of the East?

RESTFUL.

I would have thought you'd be bored. It's difficult to let go of power when you've been used to exercising it.

To settle down and grow roses up the door.

And yet here I am.

And the old firm is in new hands. And the world goes on.

That's an eighty-year-old Janneau armagnac. If I'd known you were going to waste it on melodrama I'd have given you the '78.

The world is on fire, Lucifer Morningstar. I wanted to make that point forcefully.

Otherwise we could squander the whole evening in stale repartee.

I've no desire to trespass on your evening at all, Amenadiel, I'm sure there are many places where your company would be almost welcome.

No need, Mazikeen. Leave it.

11

I am to place a proposition before you. Against my will. Against my judgment. Knowing you to be the king of liars and traitors.

Say *no* right now and you will spare me considerable effort.

There is a power at work on Earth which is granting human wishes.

SO? THERE ARE MANY SUCH. THERE HAVE ALWAYS BEEN AGENCIES THAT TRAFFIC IN THAT WAY.

Ah, but this is different. For one thing, it is new. For another, it is *growing* by increments. We have collated examples.

SHOULDN'T THIS BE ON MICROFILM?

The instances so far are trivial--treasures found in old mattresses, unexpected sexual encounters of surprising sweetness, the sudden death of rich relatives. But you know the nature of human desire.

They'll rip each other apart like rats in a sack.

12

WHY ME?

BECAUSE heaven wishes neither to intervene directly in this nor to stand by and let it happen.

YOU represent a third option. I am told that you will name your price.

THAT I *may* name my price or that I *will* name it?

Will.

YOU'D THINK PART OF OMNISCIENCE WOULD BE KNOWING WHEN TO STOP.

BUT STILL...

LIVING HERE AMONG THEM-- WATCHING THEM LIVE AND DIE AND BUILD AND BREAK--YOU CAN'T HELP BUT THINK ABOUT HOW *IMPERMANENT* EVERYTHING IS IN THIS UNIVERSE. NOTHING REALLY WORKMAN-LIKE. NOTHING MADE TO LAST.

A LETTER OF PASSAGE.

YOUR PARDON?

SAY THAT MY PRICE IS A LETTER OF PASSAGE.

AH, BUT HE'LL ALREADY *KNOW* THAT, WON'T HE?

13

I do not grasp your meaning.

IT'S NOT NECESSARY THAT YOU SHOULD.

THERE IS ANOTHER SIDE TO THE SKY, THAT'S ALL. I'M SURE THEY'LL TELL YOU ABOUT IT SOME DAY. SOME BIG, HAIRY ARCHANGEL WILL SIT YOU ON HIS LAP AND GIVE YOU THE TALK.

Your mockery demeans you. You have accepted the commission.

Do you require anything else of me before I leave?

YES. I'D LIKE AN APOLOGY.

An ap...?

FOR THE DAMAGE YOU CAUSED TO THE TABLE.

Then... in accordance with my instructions, which were to give you anything you asked for...

I apologize Lucifer Morningstar, for the damage to your table.

GOODBYE, AMENADIEL.

MAZIKEEN, TELL THE STAFF THEY CAN LEAVE. WE WILL NOT BE OPENING THIS EVENING.

YEHSZ, NGY RROAHD.

LIGHT SOME CANDLES. KEEP THEM LIT FROM NOW ON. AND BRING ME A KNIFE AND A DOVE -- ACTUALLY A PIGEON WILL DO.

OH WHERE ARE YOU GOING... SAID THE FALSE KNIGHT ON THE ROAD...

NGY RROAHD, HRRALL I NGRING HEOU A BOWL TO CASZSZ GHE VHLOOD?

THANK YOU, MAZIKEEN. NO, THE BIRD'S NOT FOR SACRIFICE. WHO WOULD I SACRIFICE IT TO?

MEMSOPH IS THE RUNE OF FINDING. IN THIS WAY THE KNIFE BECOMES A LODESTONE.

I MAY NOT KNOW WHERE I'M GOING, BUT I SEE NO REASON TO TRAVEL BLIND.

NOW YOU. DON'T BE SO FRIGHTENED. I'M NOT HUNGRY.

I'LL JUST TROUBLE YOU FOR A LOAN OF THESE. I MAY NEED TO FLY BEFORE THIS BUSINESS IS DONE WITH, AND I FORFEITED MY OWN WINGS SOME TIME SINCE.

MAZIKEEN.

YEHSZ, NGY RROAHD.

MY COAT, PLEASE. AND BRING ME MY OTHER BOTTLE. THE ONE ON THE RIGHT.

I'M GOING OUT.

DID YOU EVER EXPECT TO SEE YOUR SON AGAIN?

THERE YOU GO, SLUGGER. YOU CLEANED OUT THE WHOLE BOWL.

YOU LIKE THE CHOCOLATE ONE BEST, DON'T YOU?

NO, I ... I STOPPED HOPING WHEN I SAW THE STROLLER WAS GONE. IT'S JUST A *MIRACLE*, THAT'S ALL.

I'M GONNA LEAVE YOU AT THE WINDOW HERE. YOU CAN WATCH THOSE KIDS PLAYING.

YOU HEAR 'EM SHOUTING? NOISY LITTLE SHITHEADS.

IT'S FUNNY. YOU LOOK SO MUCH LIKE HER, BUT SHE NEVER *STOPPED* TALKING. THAT'S PROBABLY WHY I FEEL LIKE I KNOW WHAT YOUR VOICE WOULD SOUND LIKE.

ANYWAY, I'M GONNA BE BACK AROUND ELEVEN. YOU'LL BE ASLEEP THEN, SO I'LL SEE YOU IN THE *A.M.*

I'M OUTTA HERE. TALK TO 'IM A BIT, WILL YOU, FLOWER?

OKAY, DAD.

AND MOVE 'IM IN THE CHAIR ONCE IN A WHILE TO STOP 'IM GETTING SORE. SEE YOU LATER.

OKAY, LINDA. YOU'RE CLEAR TO COMMENCE APPROACH.

I'M HEARING YOU, RED LEADER. YOU WANT PRETZELS?

NAH, JUST CORN CHIPS.

I'M MOVING YOU INTO YOUR ROOM, PAUL. IT'LL BE NICE AND QUIET THERE.

LOOK, YOU'VE GOT TEDDY AND RABBIT AND SOPHIE.

OKAY?

GUY IN ROWLEYS DIDN'T EVEN LOOK AT MY I.D.

JUST AS WELL. YOU DON'T LOOK ANY-THING LIKE ARLENE DIAZ.

THAT'S WHAT LETS ME SLEEP AT NIGHT. HERE, RACHEL...

...GET HAPPY.

FAR ENOUGH, PRINCE OF HELL.

FAR ENOUGH AND A LITTLE MORE.

AH, THE HOSPITALITY OF THE LILIM! I WONDER WHAT IT DIED OF. HELLO, MAHU. HOW IS YOUR MASTER THESE DAYS?

I ACKNOWLEDGE NO MASTER.

THEN HOW IS BRIADACH THE BLIND, LORD OF THE LILIM IN EXILE? IS HE HEALTHY? I MEAN, WITHIN THE USUAL PARAMETERS?

HIS LUNGS *BURN*. HIS EVERY HEARTBEAT TEARS HIS SIDE LIKE A *FLENSING KNIFE.*

WHAT DO YOU WANT HERE, LUCIFER?

AH. WELL WITHIN THE USUAL PARAMETERS, THEN.

INFORMATION. I HAVE AN OCCASIONAL ARRANGEMENT WITH YOUR MASTER WHICH HE MAY HAVE MENTIONED TO YOU.

AN ARRANGEMENT?

AN ARRANGEMENT, YES.

THEN GO UP, AND BE DAMNED TO YOU. WHEN THE LILIM CLAIM THEIR RIGHT, YOU'LL LAST NO LONGER THAN THE ANGELS. YOU'LL JUST BURN WITH A DIFFERENT COLORED FLAME.

OH, NOTHING WILL BE BURNING BY THEN. EVEN SOLAR FUSION ONLY LASTS SO LONG.

WHO'S THERE, MANU? I HEAR VOICES.

IS IT THE CHALDAEAN BITCH, COME GRUBBING FOR NEWS OF THE DEAD CITIES? OR FALLEN SAMAEL, WITH HIS HURT PRIDE AND HIS SAVAGE TONGUE? WHO'S THERE, I SAY!

NOBODY'S CALLED ME SAMAEL FOR SUCH A LONG TIME. IT'S LIKE SOMEONE USING YOUR MAIDEN NAME.

LORD LUCIFER!

BRIADACH. STILL SICK, I SEE.

SICK? THAT'S A SHALLOW WORD TO MEASURE THE FATHOMS OF MY SUFFERING. MY LORD, IF YOU HAVE ANY OF THAT HEALING WATER ABOUT YOU I'LL TAKE IT NOW AND PAY YOU IN SOME LITTLE SPACE.

DULLS MY EYES! YOU KNOW EXACTLY WHAT I SEE. YOU KNOW EXACTLY HOW MUCH BLINDNESS HEAVEN HAS ALLOWED TO ME!

BUT IT DULLS YOUR EYES.

"THE SEED AND THE ROT." THERE'S NO NEED TO REMIND ME OF YOUR CURSE. DO YOU THINK THIS IS A SOCIAL CALL?

IF YOU WANT THE LETHE WATER, DEMON, YOU'LL HAVE TO WORK FOR IT. THE SAME RULES AS ALWAYS.

ASK ME THEN, BUT IN HELL'S NAME BE BRIEF! A BIRTH AND A DEATH. I'LL GIVE YOU TWO MOMENTS FOR TWO SIPS OF OBLIVION.

ONE MOMENT.

IT WILL BE BOTH, YOU SEE.

A BIRTH AND A DEATH.

THE BIRTH AND DEATH OF WHAT? TELL ME WHAT YOU WANT--AND LET ME HEAR YOU POUR, FOR INSPIRATION'S SAKE.

THE BIRTH AND DEATH OF A *DESIRE*. A DESIRE SATISFIED IN THE MOMENT IT'S CONCEIVED. A WISH...

...A WISH BEING GRANTED. YES, YES, I'M NOT SIMPLE. THEY'RE RARE ENOUGH SINCE MAB CLOSED HER BORDERS, BUT TODAY THEY SEEM TO BE AS COMMON AS RAIN.

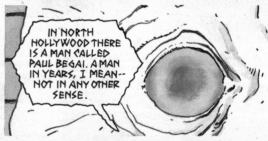

IN NORTH HOLLYWOOD THERE IS A MAN CALLED PAUL BEGAI. A MAN IN YEARS, I MEAN-- NOT IN ANY OTHER SENSE.

WHY HIM?

BECAUSE THE POWER *LINGERS* AROUND HIM. IT WINDS OVER AND THROUGH HIM.

WHAT IS IT, LUCIFER? THIS THING THAT OPENS AND OPENS AND SEEMS TO HAVE NO DEATH? HAVE YOU SEEN IT? HAVE YOU TRIED TO TALK TO IT?

NO. NOT YET. DRINK SPARINGLY, BRIADACH. I DON'T HAVE A STEADY LINE OF SUPPLY THESE DAYS.

SO KEVIN'S STILL SITTING THERE WITH HIS *DICK* OUT, BUT SUZIE'S CLIMBED OUT OF THE BATHROOM WINDOW. SHE'S HALFWAY DOWN THE STREET. AND THE LAST THING SHE HEARD HIM SAY WAS, "SUUUUZIE! I'VE GOT THE CONDOM ON!"

HAHAHAHAHA!

HEY, SUZIE SAID NO WAY ARE YOU A NAVAJO, COS NAVAJOS ARE BRIGHT RED LIKE TOMATOES. I TOLD HER TO SUCK IT.

UMM, *HALF* NAVAJO. DAD'S THE REAL THING. HE WAS BORN ON A RESERVATION. AND MY GRANDAD'S SOME KIND OF WITCH DOCTOR. SHAMAN. THING.

MMMMMUUUUH!

NNNNNNAAAAH!

KRAASH!

HEY, WHAT WAS THAT? IS THERE SOMEONE ELSE HERE?

SHIT. JUST MY BROTHER. GIVE ME A SECOND, GUYS.

YOU OKAY, PAUL?

AW, NO!

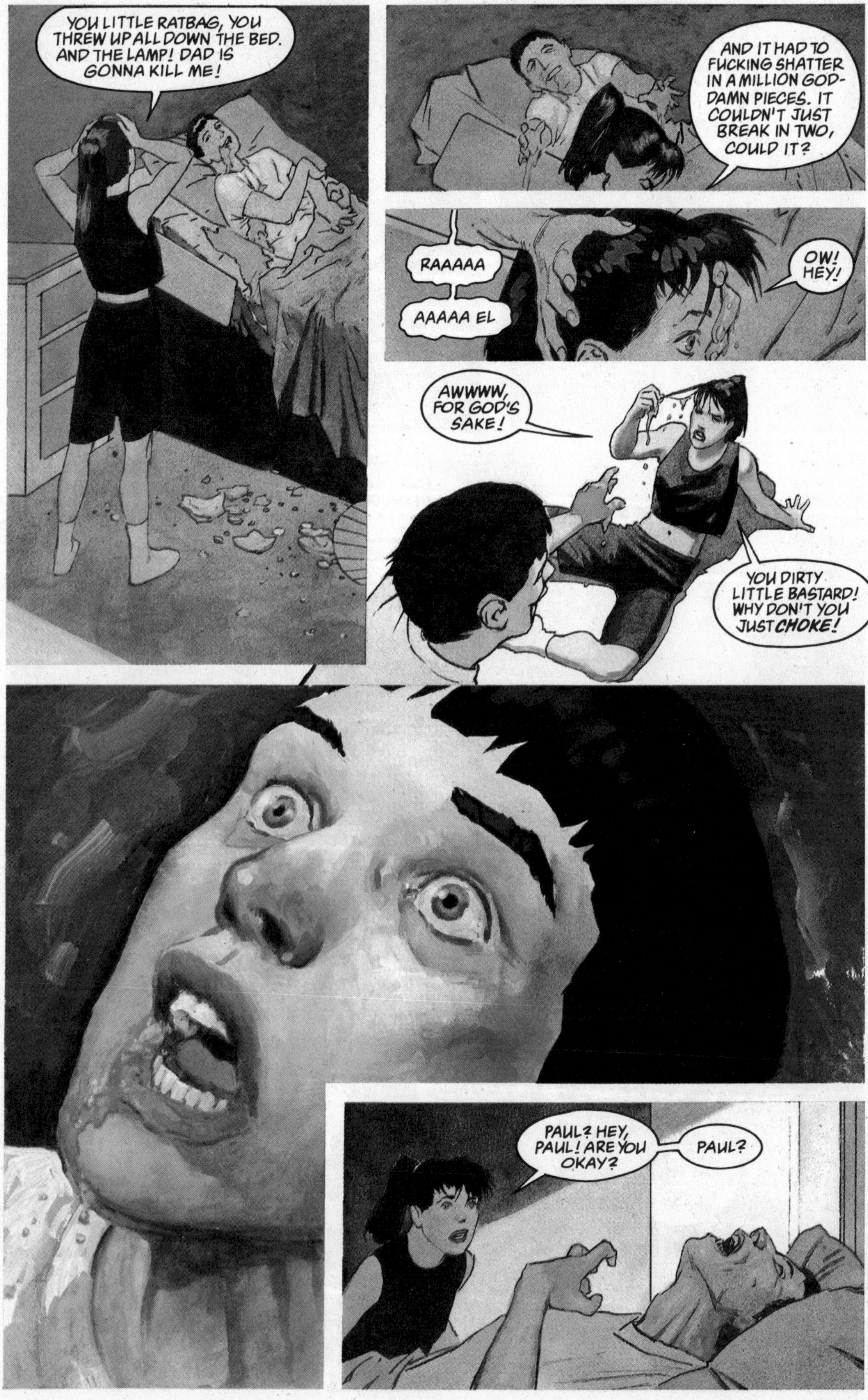
YOU LITTLE RATBAG, YOU THREW UP ALL DOWN THE BED. AND THE LAMP! DAD IS GONNA KILL ME!
AND IT HAD TO FUCKING SHATTER IN A MILLION GOD-DAMN PIECES. IT COULDN'T JUST BREAK IN TWO, COULD IT?
RAAAAA
AAAAA EL
OW! HEY!
AWWWW, FOR GOD'S SAKE!
YOU DIRTY LITTLE BASTARD! WHY DON'T YOU JUST CHOKE!
PAUL? HEY, PAUL! ARE YOU OKAY?
PAUL?

OH MY GOD! PAUL, PLEASE! DON'T DO THIS TO ME! BREATHE! PLEASE BREATHE!

EXCUSE ME. I'D LIKE TO EXAMINE HIM.

WH...? WHO ARE YOU? WHAT ARE YOU DOING?

CURIOUS. THIS WAS A MORE COMPLEX TRANSACTION THAN I THOUGHT.

AN EXCHANGE -- A TWO-WAY FLOW. POWER WAS EXPENDED HERE, BUT POWER WAS GENERATED TOO.

A VELLEITY. SOME MORON HAS CREATED A VELLEITY.

LISTEN, ARE YOU SOME KIND OF DOCTOR? ARE YOU GONNA... ARE YOU GONNA RESUSCITATE HIM?

BUT HE SAID THAT THE POWER LINGERED HERE...

COULD HE TALK?

WHAT?

YOUR BROTHER. COULD HE TALK?

NO. HE JUST... HE JUST MADE NOISES, YOU KNOW.

24

THEN PERHAPS IT'S *DRAWN* TO SILENCE. PERHAPS IT HOVERED OVER *HIM* LONG ENOUGH TO SENSE *YOUR* DESIRE.

MY WHAT?

YOUR DESIRE. WHEN YOU WISHED HIM DEAD.

WHEN I WHAT? ARE YOU CRAZY? I DIDN'T *WANT* THIS TO HAPPEN!

OF COURSE YOU DID.

YOU...YOU COLD BASTARD! HE'S MY *BROTHER!* GO TO HELL! GO STRAIGHT TO *FUCKING HELL!*

YES.

I'D BEEN HOPING TO AVOID THAT. BUT YOU'RE RIGHT. THERE'S NO GETTING AROUND IT, IS THERE?

HEY! HEY, WHERE ARE YOU? WHERE DID YOU GO?

OH GODDDDDD!

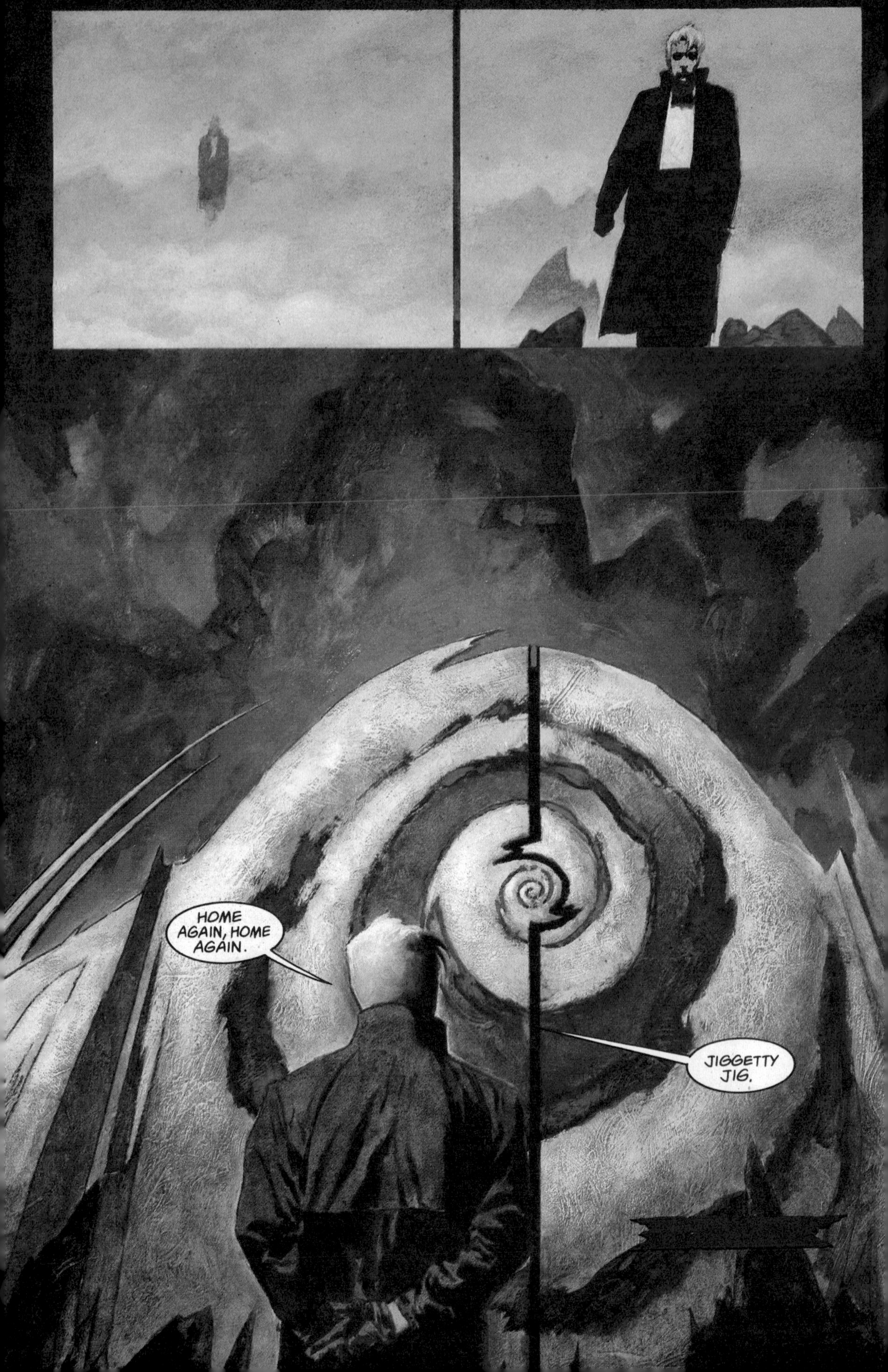
HOME AGAIN, HOME AGAIN.
JIGGETTY JIG.

THE CUP IS EMPTY. HARD TO REMEMBER THE *COMFORT* IT HELD. ALL GONE NOW. ALL DRIED UP.

BRIADACH SETS HIS TEETH IN THE HOT DUSK. THE BLINDFOLD IS NO HELP TONIGHT. HE IS ASSAILED BY *IMAGES*. SEEDS. BEGINNINGS. GAPING MOUTHS THAT ISSUE FORTH THE ENDLESS SPEW OF FUTURE TIME.

I WISH I MAY, I WISH I MIGHT... A SWEET POISON IS SPREADING OUT ACROSS THE EARTH.

DANNY FOLGER IS A CROUPIER, BUT NOT AFTER TONIGHT. NO MATTER HOW FAST HE SLAMS THE BRAKE, THE WHEEL IS FASTER. THE LAW OF PROBABILITY JUST TURNED AND *BIT* HIM IN THE HAND.

BRENDA LIMOTO FINDS HER WEDDING RING, WHICH SHE GAVE UP FOR LOST SIX YEARS AGO, INSIDE THE HOLE IN THE WALL THAT SHE FINALLY DECIDED TO PLASTER.

HYDRANTS BURST IN EVERY DOWNTOWN AREA. STREET PUNKS DANCE IN THE SPRAY LIKE A SCENE FROM SOME CORNY MOVIE.

I WISH I MAY...

AND *LUCIFER*, HEAVEN'S FALLEN AGENT...

...WALKING THE ROCKY PATHS OF THE NINTH CIRCLE, SURROUNDED BY HORRORS AS WIDE AND VARIOUS AS THE HUMAN MIND CAN HOLD...

...EVEN LUCIFER IS COMING *HOME*.

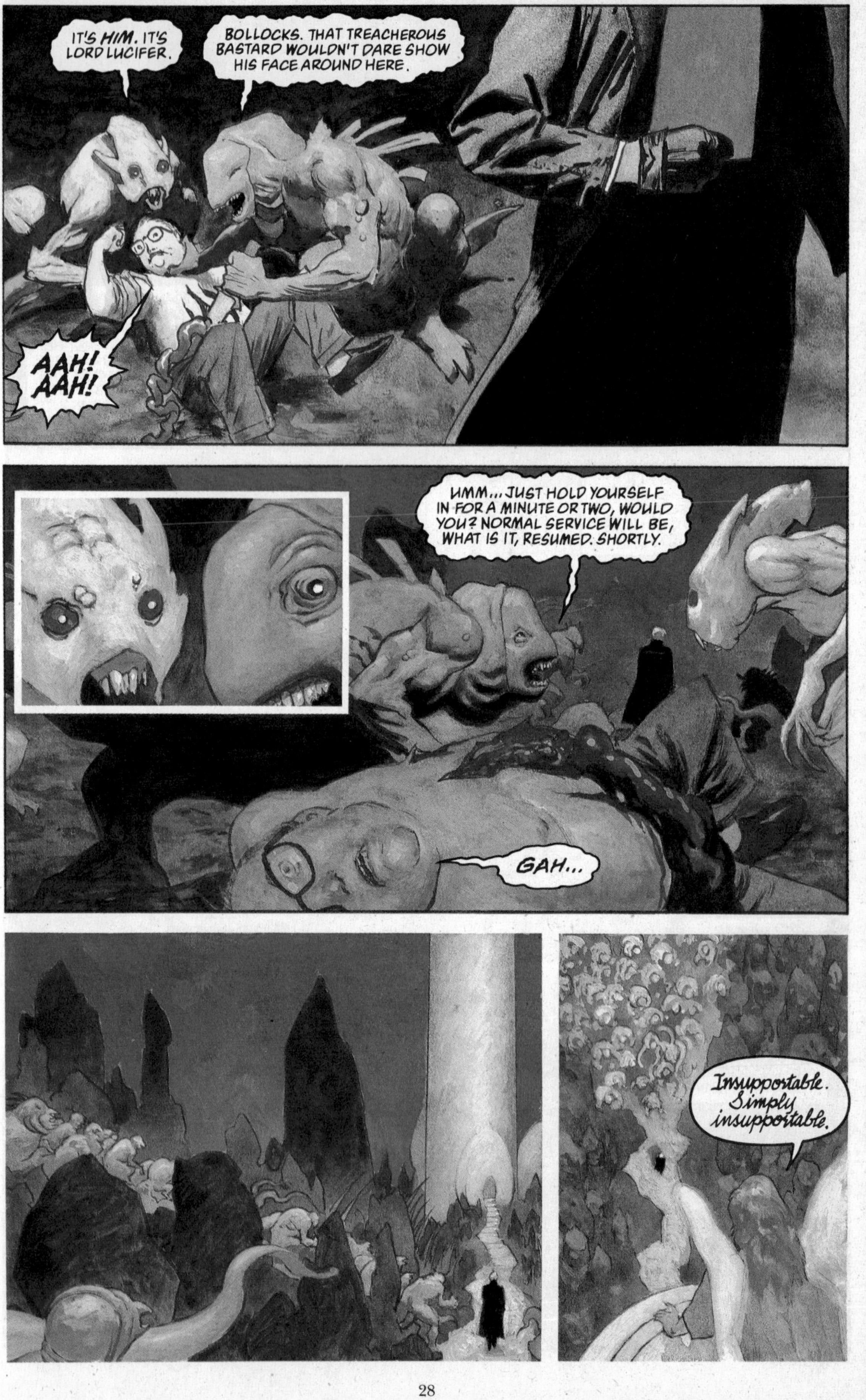

IT'S HIM. IT'S LORD LUCIFER.
BOLLOCKS. THAT TREACHEROUS BASTARD WOULDN'T DARE SHOW HIS FACE AROUND HERE.
AAH! AAH!
UMM... JUST HOLD YOURSELF IN FOR A MINUTE OR TWO, WOULD YOU? NORMAL SERVICE WILL BE, WHAT IS IT, RESUMED. SHORTLY.
GAH...
Insupportable. Simply insupportable.

LITTLE PIG, LITTLE PIG, LET ME IN.

This is no longer your domain, Lucifer Morningstar. You have no right of entry here. No right even to walk on this ground without our leave.

HMM. IN MY DAY WE TOOK IN ANYONE WHO HAPPENED BY. THAT'S PART OF THE POINT, ISN'T IT?

You will not face me down and you will not sway me. Our work of redemption is at a delicate stage, and your presence here drags everything back into question.

REMIEL, YOU ONCE BEGGED ME TO RETURN...

I HAVEN'T FINISHED YET!

OH WELL.

You come here with all your old arrogance — like a visiting head of state, when the truth is you've evaded your responsibilities. You resigned.

You resigned, Lucifer.

YOUR GRASP OF CURRENT AFFAIRS IS AS KEEN AS EVER.

Spare me your sarcasm. I have nothing more to say to you.

REMIEL...

HOW MANY DEMONS STAND BEHIND US? I RECKON AT LEAST A THIRD OF THE INFERNAL HOST.

IF YOU DON'T LET ME COME INSIDE I'LL HUMILIATE YOU SO BADLY THAT YOUR PRESTIGE HERE — WHICH I IMAGINE IS ALSO AT A DELICATE STAGE — WILL CATCH COLD AND DIE.

GOOD LAD. ALWAYS KNOW YOUR LIMITATIONS, EH?

AND WHY AM I SEEING THIS, BRIADACH WONDERS.

RACHEL BEGAI, FIFTEEN MINUTES AFTER HER BROTHER'S DEATH.

WHAT SEED OPENS HERE?

AHUH. AHUH. AHUH.

THAT'S OKAY, RACHEL. LET IT OUT.

SHE IS LETTING IT OUT, LINDA. SHE'S BEEN CRYING FOR A QUARTER OF AN HOUR.

I'M ONLY TRYING TO HELP, XIMENA.

I THINK I GOT THE VOMIT OUT OF THE SHEET. SHOULD I HANG IT ON A RADIATOR?

WHAT ARE YOU EVEN BOTHERING WITH THE FUCKING SHEET FOR? YOU'RE NOT SUPPOSED TO TOUCH ANYTHING!

I DIDN'T... I ONLY...

THE COPS WILL PROBABLY HAUL YOU IN FOR TAMPERING WITH THE EVIDENCE.

I DON'T THINK WE CALLED THE COPS YET, DID WE?

DID YOU GUYS CALL THE COPS?

WE CAN'T. MY DAD'S GONNA KILL ME FOR THIS.

PAUL'S DEAD, AND I WAS HAVING A.... A PARTY. AHUH. AHUH.

BONG CLANG

OH NO.

WELL I GUESS SOMEONE CALLED 'EM.

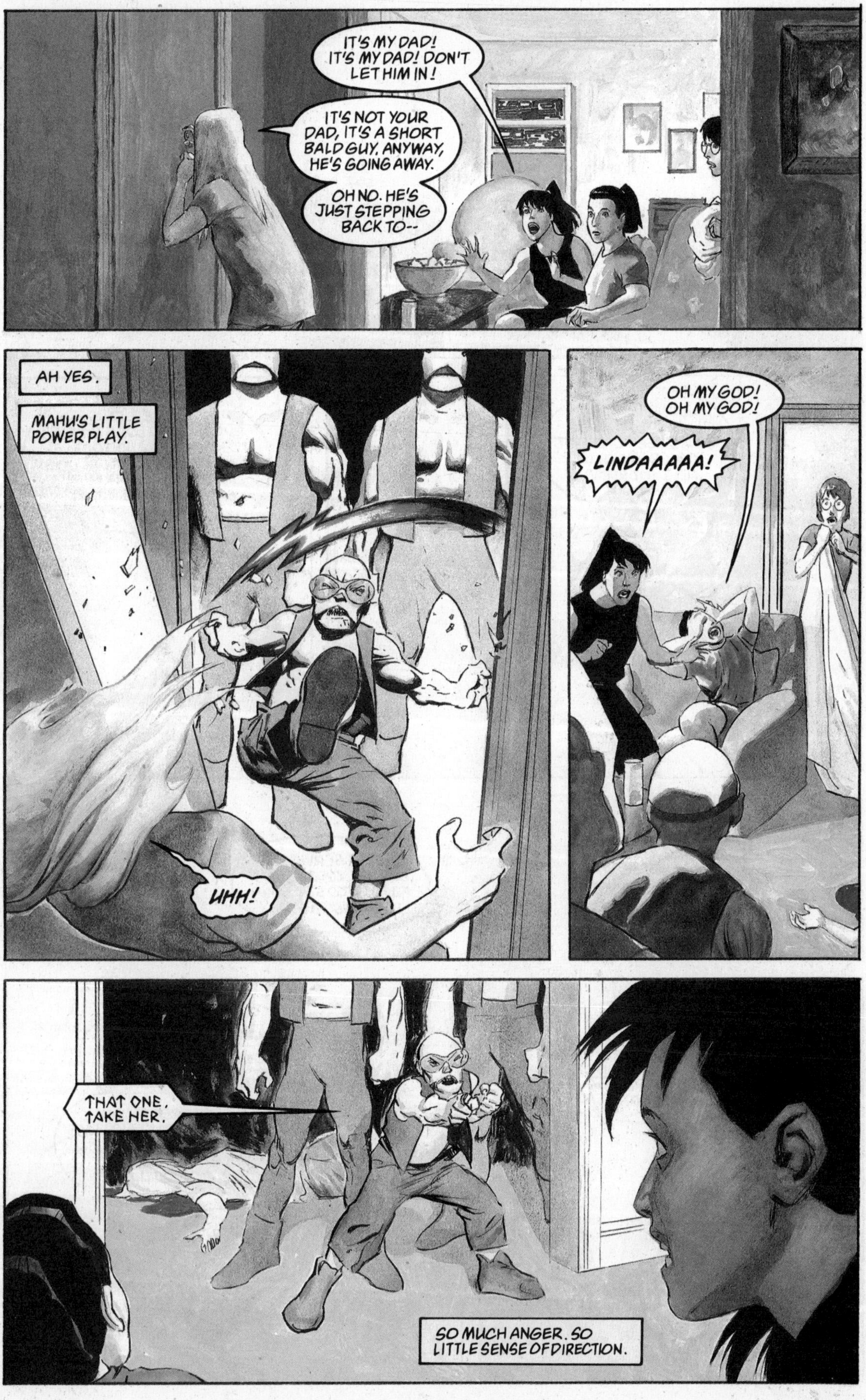
IT'S MY DAD! IT'S MY DAD! DON'T LET HIM IN!
IT'S NOT YOUR DAD, IT'S A SHORT BALD GUY. ANYWAY, HE'S GOING AWAY.
OH NO. HE'S JUST STEPPING BACK TO--
AH YES.
MAHU'S LITTLE POWER PLAY.
UHH!
OH MY GOD! OH MY GOD!
LINDAAAAAA!
THAT ONE. TAKE HER.
SO MUCH ANGER. SO LITTLE SENSE OF DIRECTION.

"ANNIHILATING ALL THAT'S MADE, TO A GREEN THOUGHT IN A GREEN SHADE." DO I INTRUDE, DUMA?

I CARRIED THIS BURDEN FOR LONG ENOUGH TO KNOW HOW IRKSOME IT CAN BE. NOR WOULD I TRESPASS HERE NOW EXCEPT THAT I AM IN THE SERVICE OF...

...THE SERVICE OF HEAVEN. THAT WAS HARDER TO SAY THAN I'D ANTICIPATED.

BEFORE YOU TOOK UP YOUR PLACE HERE YOU WERE A TUTELARY SPIRIT. YOU HAD CARE OF SILENCE. IT'S IN THAT CAPACITY THAT I COME TO YOU NOW.

I WAS NEVER A GUARDIAN, OF COURSE, BUT I ALWAYS FELT THAT YOU GOT THE SHITTY END OF THE STICK.

ADAM'S CHILDREN ALLOW SO LITTLE ROOM IN THEIR LIVES FOR SILENCE--AND YET DESPITE ITS RARITY THEY SEEM INCAPABLE OF VALUING IT.

BUT THERE WERE AGES OF SILENCE. DO YOU REMEMBER, DUMA? BEFORE THEY CRAWLED OUT OF THE SEA--WHEN YOU COULD STILL HEAR YOURSELF THINK?

MY OWN TASTES TEND MORE TO THE BAROQUE, BUT I DID APPRECIATE THAT...

AND EVEN WHEN THE HOMINIDS ARRIVED THEY COULDN'T SPEAK, OF COURSE. SO THEY WERE STILL YOUR CHARGES.

YOUR GOLDEN AGE, WASN'T IT? MINE TOO. WHEN THE GAS CLOUDS WERE COALESCING INTO SUNS AND I WAS GOD'S LAMP-LIGHTER.

I DID DROP IN ON THE EARTH, ONCE IN A WHILE. I REMEMBER THE SILENCE--LIKE AN OCEAN WITH NO TIDES.

AND THE LITTLE GODS. THEY FLOATED IN THE AIR LIKE FLIES. THAT BRINGS ME TO MY POINT, ACTUALLY.

"THE POOR, NAKED HALF-MEN, SCARED OF THEIR OWN SHADOWS...THEY MADE THE BEST GODS THEY COULD, BUT THEY HAD NO LANGUAGE TO GIVE SHAPE TO THEIR IMAGININGS. SO THE FIRST GODS WERE THIN GRAY SHADOWS, WITH-OUT FORM AND WITHOUT SPEECH, DREDGED INTO BEING BY THE DUMB LONGINGS OF THEIR WORSHIPPERS."

"FOR THREE HUNDRED THOUSAND YEARS THESE SHADOW THINGS WERE THE ONLY PANTHEON THERE WAS. WE CALLED THEM THE VOICELESS GODS. THEN WE IGNORED THEM.

"WHEN THE OTHERS CAME ALONG, THE GODS WITH THE FIRM HANDSHAKES, IT WAS EASY TO FORGET ABOUT THE LITTLE SILENT ONES."

BUT IT WOULDN'T TAKE MUCH TO KEEP THEM GOING. JUST THE OCCASION-AL HEARTFELT PRAYER TO NOBODY IN PARTICULAR, THE "OH THANK GODS" OF PEOPLE WHO DON'T REALLY KNOW WHICH GOD THEY MEAN.

THEY'RE STILL THERE, AREN'T THEY, DUMA?

AND NOW THERE'S A POWER LOOSE ON THE EARTH THAT MANIFESTS ITSELF IN SILENCE-- THAT SEEMS DRAWN TO SILENCE.

A VELLEITY. I RECOGNIZED IT BECAUSE I MADE ONE MYSELF ONCE, WHEN I HAD LESS PATIENCE AND LESS FORESIGHT.

BUT THIS ONE BELONGS TO THEM. THE VOICELESS ONES. PERHAPS THE GENERAL WASH OF BELIEF AS THE NEW MILLENNIUM APPROACHES GAVE THEM THE INITIAL SURGE OF POWER TO MAKE THE WEAVING.

IT'S A DANGEROUS MAGIC, DUMA. IT GRANTS WISHES AND ACCUMULATES POWER FROM THE WISHER'S FEELINGS OF GRATITUDE OR GUILT. IT GETS BIG- GER ALL THE TIME.

THE SPELL MUST BE UNWOVEN BEFORE IT DEVOURS THE WORLD. PLEASE. TELL ME WHERE I HAVE TO GO TO FIND THEM.

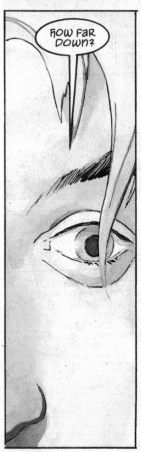

HOW FAR DOWN?

I SEE.

THANK YOU, DUMA.

"DO YOU HAVE ANY *ENEMIES*, MR. BEGAI? ANYONE WITH A GRUDGE AGAINST YOU?"

"DO YOU OWE *MONEY* TO ANYONE?"

NO, I CAN'T THINK OF ANYONE WHO'D... WHO COULD...

JESUS CHRIST. I DON'T BELIEVE THIS IS HAPPENING.

WELL, CAN YOU AT LEAST TELL ME YOUR DAUGHTER'S BLOOD TYPE?

YEAH. SHE WAS B NEGATIVE, LIKE HER MOTHER. WHY DO YOU...?

THEN THE BLOOD IN THE FOOTPRINTS BELONGS TO THE FRIEND, LINDA MALPASS. THAT'S GOOD NEWS, I GUESS.

BUT YOU'D BETTER FACE IT, MR. BEGAI. THEY *KNEW* WHAT THEY WANTED, AND WHAT THEY WANTED WAS YOUR DAUGHTER.

NOW ONE OF THE WITNESSES IS DEAD, AND THE OTHER TWO ARE UNDER SEDATION.

IF YOU WANT RACHEL BACK IN ONE PIECE, THEN FOR GOD'S SAKE *THINK*. IS THERE *ANYTHING* YOU CAN TELL ME THAT WOULD NARROW DOWN THE SEARCH AT LEAST A LITTLE?

NO.

HELLO. I WISH TO SPEAK TO YOUR MR. FARRELL, PLEASE. I BELIEVE HE IS IN CHARGE OF TRANSPORTATION.

YES, WE'VE HAD DEALINGS BEFORE. TELL HIM IT'S SAM.

PHARAMOND? YES, IT'S ME. JUST FINE, THANKS. WELL, ACTUALLY, I NEED YOU TO ARRANGE ME A PASSAGE TO,...AH.

I'LL HAVE TO CALL YOU BACK.

I'M DISAPPOINTED IN YOU, LUCIFER MORNINGSTAR.

I'D TAKE IT AS A FAVOR IF YOU'D GET TO THE POINT. THIS IS AN AWKWARD TIME.

THE GREAT REVOLUTIONARY TURNED INTO HEAVEN'S HANDMAID. I RESPECTED YOU. I DIDN'T LIKE YOU, BUT I RESPECTED YOU. BUT NOW,... PFAH!

TELL ME, COLLABORATOR. THIS GREAT WEAVING --THIS VELLEITY. WHAT WILL IT DO FOR US?

WHY, IT WILL MAKE YOUR DREAMS COME TRUE, MAHU. UGLY AS THAT SOUNDS.

36

MY DREAMS ARE IRRELEVANT. I CLAIM THIS MAGIC FOR THE ARMIES OF THE LILIM IN EXILE. GIVE IT TO ME AND YOU CAN HAVE THE GIRL BACK UNHARMED.

HMM? WHAT GIRL WOULD THAT BE?

THE HALF-CASTE. RACHEL BEGAI. I FOLLOWED YOU THERE, LUCIFER. I KNOW EVERYWHERE YOU WENT AND EVERYTHING YOU DID.

THEN HOW COULD YOU MISS THE POINT SO SPECTACULARLY? THE GIRL'S OF NO IMPORTANCE. OH, SOME SLIGHT SPARK OF POWER, PERHAPS, BUT IN HERSELF...NOTHING.

LUX

STILL, THERE ARE SYNCHRONICITIES OPERATING HERE.

PERHAPS... YES.

THEN YOU AGREE TO MY TERMS?

OF COURSE NOT.

TSSSS

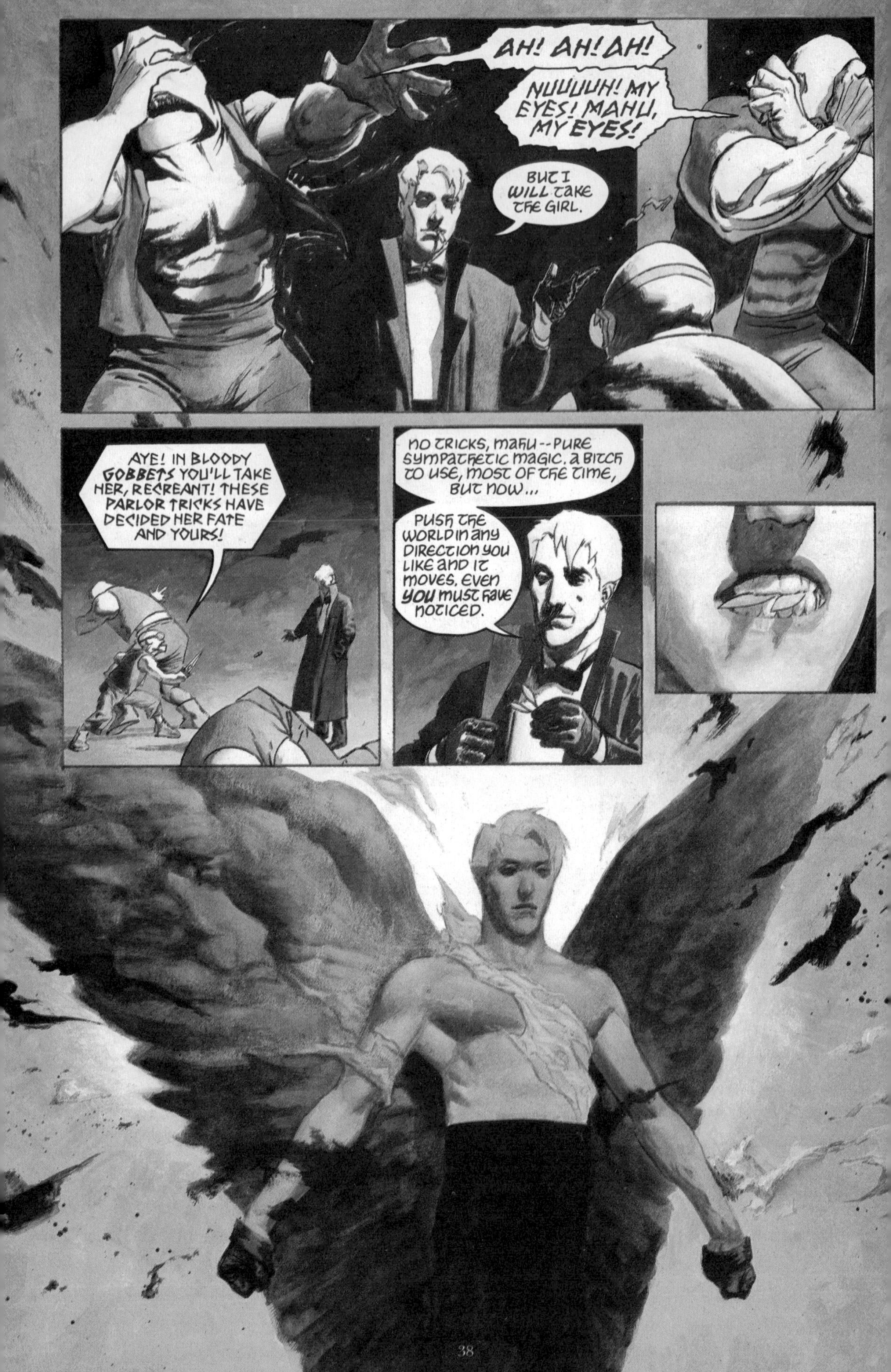
AH! AH! AH!
NUUUUH! MY EYES! MAHU, MY EYES!
BUT I WILL TAKE THE GIRL.
AYE! IN BLOODY GOBBETS YOU'LL TAKE HER, RECREANT! THESE PARLOR TRICKS HAVE DECIDED HER FATE AND YOURS!
NO TRICKS, MAHU--PURE SYMPATHETIC MAGIC. A BITCH TO USE, MOST OF THE TIME, BUT NOW...
PUSH THE WORLD IN ANY DIRECTION YOU LIKE AND IT MOVES. EVEN YOU MUST HAVE NOTICED.

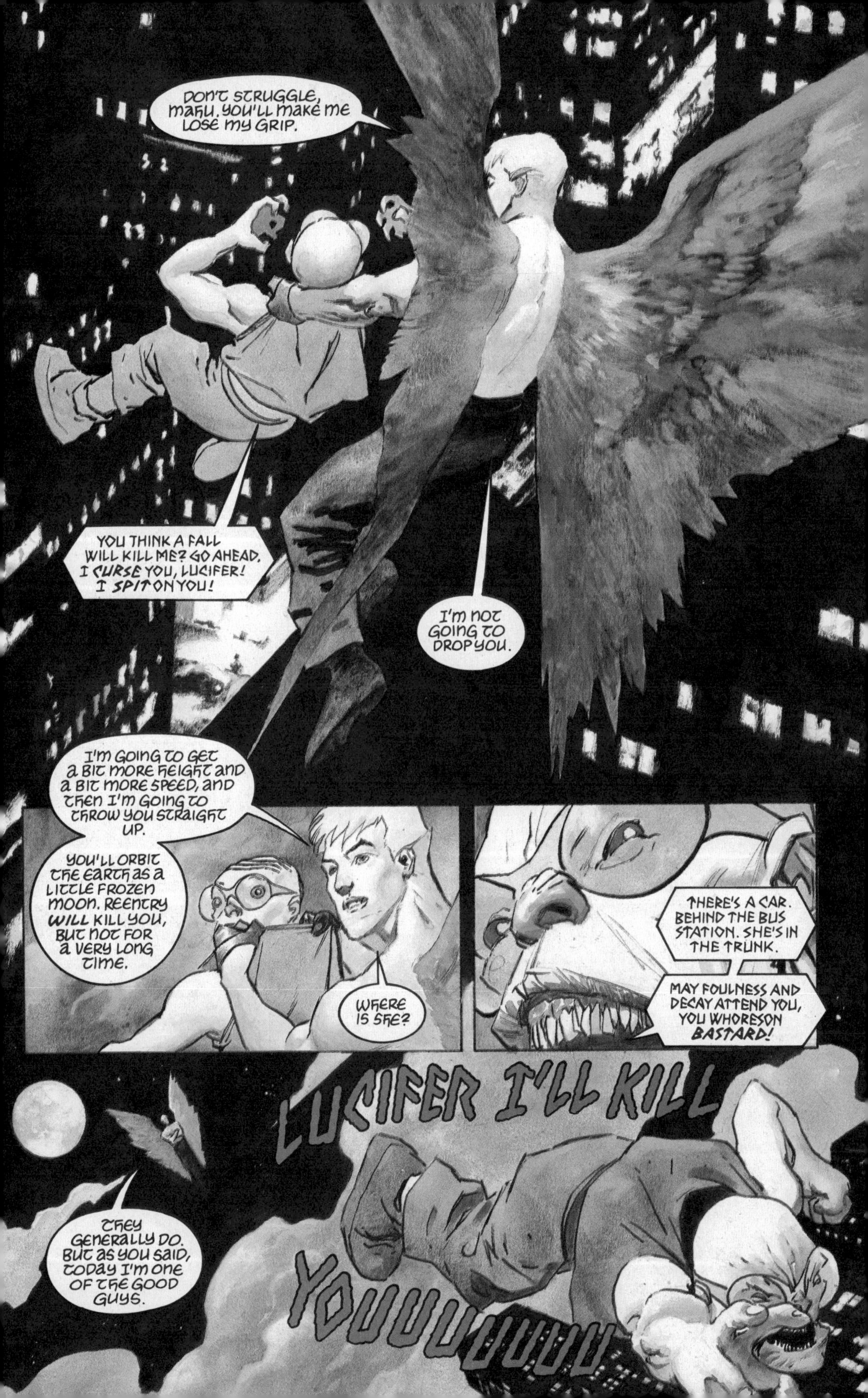
DON'T STRUGGLE, MAHU. YOU'LL MAKE ME LOSE MY GRIP.
YOU THINK A FALL WILL KILL ME? GO AHEAD. I CURSE YOU, LUCIFER! I SPIT ON YOU!
I'M NOT GOING TO DROP YOU.
I'M GOING TO GET A BIT MORE HEIGHT AND A BIT MORE SPEED, AND THEN I'M GOING TO THROW YOU STRAIGHT UP.
YOU'LL ORBIT THE EARTH AS A LITTLE FROZEN MOON. REENTRY WILL KILL YOU, BUT NOT FOR A VERY LONG TIME.
WHERE IS SHE?
THERE'S A CAR. BEHIND THE BUS STATION. SHE'S IN THE TRUNK.
MAY FOULNESS AND DECAY ATTEND YOU, YOU WHORESON BASTARD!
LUCIFER I'LL KILL YOUUUUUUU
THEY GENERALLY DO. BUT AS YOU SAID, TODAY I'M ONE OF THE GOOD GUYS.

"AND NOW THERE'S A POWER LOOSE ON THE EARTH THAT MANIFESTS ITSELF IN SILENCE..."

"IT'S A DANGEROUS MAGIC..."

MAZIKEEN, I SHALL REQUIRE YOUR ASSISTANCE.

I C'N WALK. PUT ME DOWN.

I HOPE THAT SHOW OF BRAVADO ISN'T MEANT TO BE ENDEARING. MAZI-KEEN, SOMETHING RESTORATIVE -- AND QUICKLY, PLEASE.

HMMM. YES. SOME POWER THERE, PERHAPS, IF WE HAD TIME TO SIT AND TEASE IT OUT. NEVER MIND.

MAZIKEEN?

OH. I SEE.

VERY WELL. I PRESUME THAT POSSES-SING HER IS A MEANS OF SPEAKING TO ME.

I'M LISTENING, BRIEFLY.

RELENT

A MESSAGE WRITTEN IN BLOOD. EVERYONE INVOLVED IN THIS DRAMA SEEMS COMPELLED TO OVERACT.

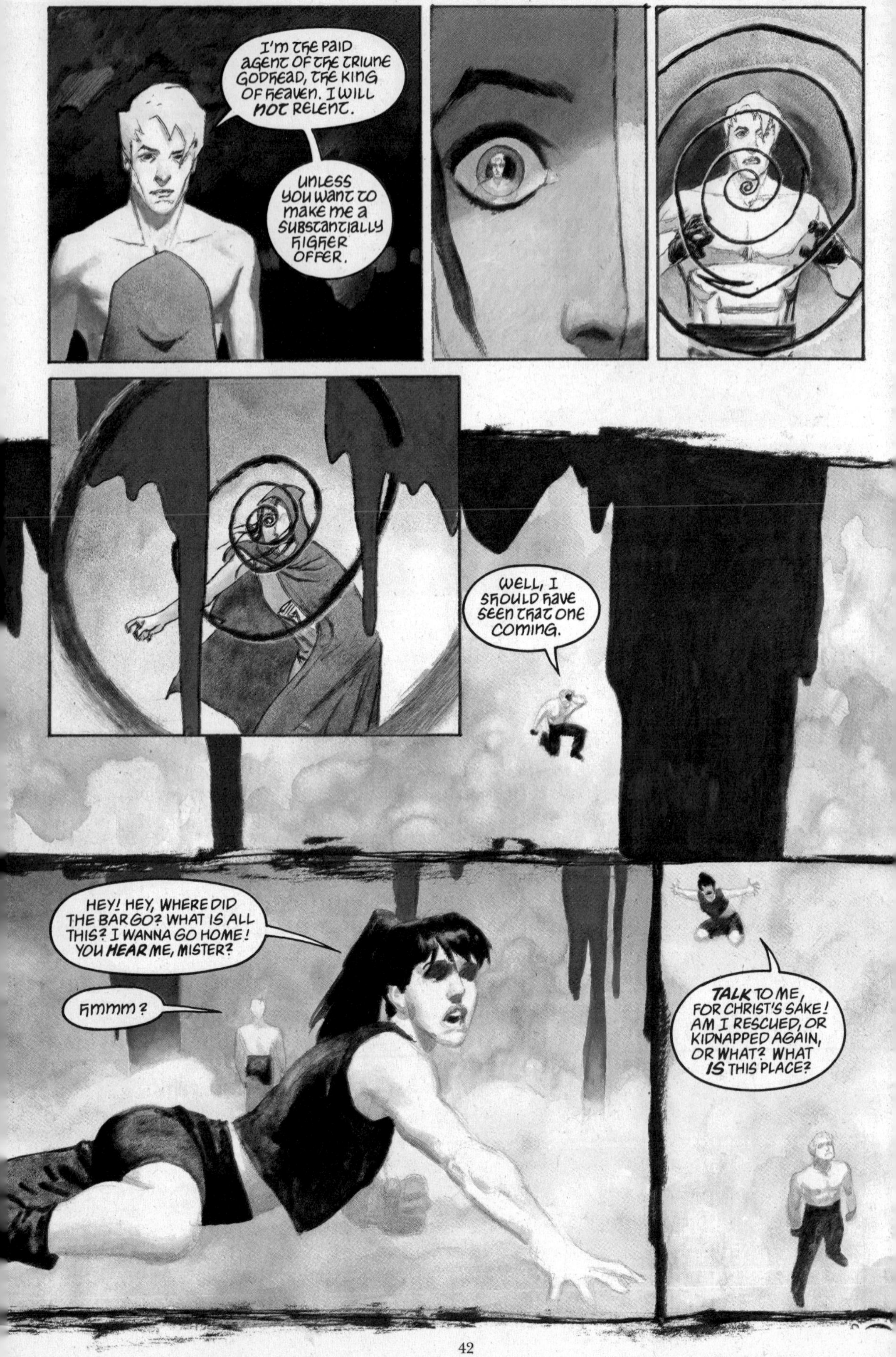
I'M THE PAID AGENT OF THE TRIUNE GODHEAD, THE KING OF HEAVEN. I WILL NOT RELENT.
UNLESS YOU WANT TO MAKE ME A SUBSTANTIALLY HIGHER OFFER.
WELL, I SHOULD HAVE SEEN THAT ONE COMING.
HEY! HEY, WHERE DID THE BAR GO? WHAT IS ALL THIS? I WANNA GO HOME! YOU HEAR ME, MISTER?
HMMM?
TALK TO ME, FOR CHRIST'S SAKE! AM I RESCUED, OR KIDNAPPED AGAIN, OR WHAT? WHAT IS THIS PLACE?

RELENT

THE REFLECTION OF A REFLECTION.

MORE SPECIFICALLY, THE REFLECTION OF MAZIKEEN'S EYE ONTO THE SURFACE OF THE BAR MIRROR. A REALITY TRAP.

THAT DOESN'T MAKE ANY...

BE QUIET, CHILD, AND LET ME THINK.

THIS IS SERIOUS. WE'RE TWO LEVELS ABSTRACTED FROM REALITY, SO THE RUNE OF FINDING IS UNLIKELY TO WORK.

I COULD TEAR US A WAY OUT, GIVEN TIME. GIVEN TIME IN GEOLOGICAL AMOUNTS.

THAT'S IT! IT'S THE BAR! CAN WE JUST BREAK THROUGH HERE SOMEHOW?

NO. IF IT WERE THAT EASY I'D HAVE DONE IT ALREADY.

BUT THIS IS MAZIKEEN'S BLOOD. WE'LL JUST HAVE TO HOPE IT KNOWS ITS WAY HOME.

BLOOD? THIS IS BLOOD?

WHY DIDN'T YOU TELL ME THAT BEFORE I TOUCHED IT?

43

COME.

YOU KEEP YOUR HANDS TO YOURSELF, PAL!

I'M COMING, BUT I'LL TELL YOU THIS MUCH -- SOON AS I'M OUT OF HERE, I'M ON THE PHONE AND THE COPS'LL BE ALL OVER YOUR PEDOPHILE KID-NAP RING ASS!

STAY IN THE CENTER OF THE CORRIDOR.

DON'T TOUCH ANYTHING. AND IF ANYTHING SPEAKS TO YOU, DON'T ANSWER.

UMM... MAYBE THAT WAS OUT OF ORDER. I APOLOGIZE. FOR THE PEDOPHILE BIT, ANYWAY.

IT'S NOT IMPORTANT.

I MEAN, I KNOW YOU SAVED ME FROM THOSE GUYS. I'M JUST FREAKED OUT, IS ALL.

SO HEY. ARE THESE THINGS DANGEROUS?

EVERYTHING THAT LIVES BETWEEN THE WORLDS IS DANGEROUS.

OH. RIGHT.

ARE WE GONNA GET A DOCTOR FOR YOUR FRIEND?

A DOCTOR CAN'T HELP HER. IF WE SUCCEED IN OUR MISSION SHE'LL RECOVER.

OUR MISSION? SINCE WHEN DID I HAVE A MISSION?

DO YOU WANT YOUR BROTHER BACK?

WHAT? YEAH. YEAH, OF COURSE I DO. BUT HE'S DEAD.

IF YOU STAY WITH ME YOU WILL HAVE ONE CHANCE TO MAKE HIM LIVE AGAIN.

OH FUCK.

WELL, LOOK... CAN I JUST PHONE MY DAD?

TELL HIM I'M OKAY? HE PROBABLY THINKS I'M DEAD OR SOMETHING.

AT THIS STAGE...

...IT'S PROBABLY BETTER NOT TO GET HIS HOPES UP.

44

MASTER, FORGIVE ME. I ACTED UNWISELY AND WITHOUT YOUR BLESSING.

YOU ACTED LIKE AN IMBECILE. BUT THAT'S REASSURING, IN ITS WAY. IN A UNIVERSE OF FLUX, SOME THINGS ARE STABLE.

HE WOULD NOT BARGAIN WITH US. HE TOOK THE GIRL. TOOK TREACHEROUS ADVANTAGE RATHER THAN FIGHTING...FIGHTING ME FAIRLY...

I KNOW. IT DOESN'T MATTER. THIS POWER IS NOT A TOOL TO BE USED.

THE WORLD...MAHU, THE WORLD IS BEGINNING TO MELT. ALREADY THE DEAD RETURN, AND THE MAPS REDRAW THEMSELVES TO ACCOMMODATE THE LANDS THAT NEVER WERE.

THE LANDS THAT...?

YES, YES, YOU KNOW. ALL THE GREATER ISRAELS AND PALESTINES. THE IRELANDS UNITED AND DIVIDED. THE SWEATSTAIN PRINCIPALITIES OF EASTERN EUROPE WHOSE NAMES WERE MERCIFULLY ERASED FROM HISTORY.

OR PERHAPS YOU DON'T KNOW. YOU'VE LET A LOT OF THE LAST QUARTER OF A MILLION YEARS GO RIGHT OVER YOUR HEAD, HAVEN'T YOU?

WE'RE AT WAR! ARE WE NOT AT WAR? WHAT TIME DO I HAVE TO WATCH THEIR PETTY AFFAIRS WHEN I CONTEND WITH HEAVEN AND HELL?

WELL, YOUR WAR IS MOOT, HEAVEN'S BREACHED, AND HELL'S AN EMPTY GESTURE.

WHEN THE WORLD AND DESIRE BECOME ONE ...

"...THERE WILL BE NO NEED OF A SEPARATE PLACE CALLED HELL."

I BEG YOUR PARDON, LORD MORNINGSTAR, MISS BEGAI... I DON'T NORMALLY TAKE BREAKFAST IN THE OFFICE, BUT TONIGHT I HAVE NOT BEEN HOME.

A NUMBER OF MY ENTERPRISES HAVE BEEN ...HOW SHALL I PUT IT... DISRUPTED TONIGHT, IN SMALL BUT ANNOYING WAYS. IT WAS NECESSARY FOR ME TO OVERSEE MANY THINGS PERSONALLY.

MAY I POUR SOME MORE TEA FOR EITHER OF YOU?

NO THANK YOU, PHARAMOND.

PLEASE. I PREFER IN THIS PLACE TO BE CALLED FARRELL.

AND YOU, LORD LUCIFER? WHAT NAME DO YOU GO BY THESE DAYS?

SPOOF!

LUCIFER! HAHAHA!

YEAH, RIGHT.

I HONESTLY DON'T CARE, NOT "LORD," THOUGH. IT'S ANACHRONISTIC.

YES, I HAD HEARD THAT YOU RESIGNED YOUR OFFICE. I WAS SORRY, ON THE WHOLE.

CHANGES IN ANCIENT ORDERS DEPRESS ME MORE AS I GROW MORE ANCIENT MYSELF.

YOU...YOU'RE REALLY HIM? JESUS.

AAAAH, SORRY. I MEAN... WHAT'S THE DEAL WITH PAUL? YOU TOOK HIS SOUL, AND NOW I'VE GOTTA PLAY SOME KIND OF GAME WITH YOU TO GET HIM BACK?

NO, THAT'S NOT THE DEAL.

PHARAMOND, WE NEED PASSAGE AND A GUIDE TO FIRST WORLD. HOW SOON CAN THAT BE ARRANGED?

FUCK.

HAH. YOU ASK HOW SOON. EVEN IN NORMAL TIMES, I FIND THIS HARD TO ANSWER. YOU UNDERSTAND, MY FRIEND,...

...SUCH JOURNEYS ARE ALWAYS AT LEAST PARTLY SHAMANISTIC. IT'S HARD, THERE-FORE, TO GUARANTEE SUCCESS. OR EVEN SURVIVAL.

I DIDN'T ASK FOR ANY GUARANTEES.

TRUE. BUT THEN THE MATTER OF *PAYMENT* BECOMES PROBLEMATIC. THE SITUATION IS NOT PROPITIOUS, AND THE ARRANGEMENTS INVOLVED ARE,...

TWO HUNDRED AND FORTY COPPER AES, COLLECTED IN THE USUAL WAY. YOU MAY COUNT THEM, ALTHOUGH TO DO SO WILL LIMIT THEIR USEFULNESS.

THERE IS TRUST BETWEEN US, MORNINGSTAR. I DON'T *NEED* TO COUNT THEM.

RACHEL, YOU ARE NAVAJO, YES?

WELL, PART NAVAJO. MY DAD IS,...

HER FATHER IS BORN TO THE FEATHER CLAN AND BORN FOR THE MANY HOGANS CLAN. HER MOTHER IS NOT OF THE DINEH. WHY DO YOU ASK?

YOU CAN GO TO TSOODZIL.

HOW'D YOU KNOW ALL THAT STUFF ABOUT US?

MY DAD'S CLAN AND ALL. EVEN I DIDN'T KNOW THAT.

THE WORLD IS A BOOK. SOME WORDS STAND OUT FROM THE PAGE.

COMPLIMENTS OF MR. FARRELL, SIR. WHERE TO?

THANK YOU. LAX, PLEASE.

THAT'S NOT AN ANSWER. AND WHAT'S WITH THE CAR? CAN'T YOU JUST DO THE DOOR-OUT-OF-BLOOD THING AGAIN?

THIS IS A PILGRIMAGE. THERE ARE PROTOCOLS.

PLEASE PHONE AHEAD AND BOOK US ON A FLIGHT TO ALBUQUERQUE.

I BELIEVE MR. FARRELL HAS ALREADY TAKEN CARE OF THAT, SIR.

AND WHY EXACTLY ARE WE GOING TO ALBUQUERQUE?

I KNOW NEW MEXICO'S A HELLHOLE BUT I DON'T BELIEVE MY BROTHER WENT THERE WHEN HE DIED.

YOU REALLY HAVE NO KNOWLEDGE OF YOUR OWN HERITAGE AT ALL, DO YOU?

NEVER MIND. WE'RE ON HEAVEN'S BUSINESS, GIRL. THE ONE JOB THAT CAN'T BE LEFT TO THE REGULAR STAFF.

WE'RE GOING TO KILL SOME GODS.

"I'M *REALLY SORRY*," THE RECEPTIONIST SAID. "UNLESS THERE'S SOME KIND OF EMERGENCY..."

"YEAH, THERE IS," RACHEL WANTED TO SAY. "WE'RE GOING TO SAVE THE *WORLD*. ME AND LUCIFER HERE. THERE ARE THESE *GODS* WHO ARE FUCKING WITH PEOPLE'S HEART'S DESIRE AND WE'RE GONNA KILL THEM."

BUT "NO," HE SAID. "IT'S JUST A VISIT. IT CAN WAIT."

WHAT DID YOU SAY *THAT* FOR? I THOUGHT...

IF ALL REGULAR FLIGHTS ARE SUSPENDED, I CAN ONLY GET US ONTO A PLANE BY LIES OR COERCION. AS I'VE ALREADY SAID, THIS IS A SHAMANISTIC JOURNEY.

LIES AND COERCION WOULD HURT OUR CHANCES OF SUCCESS.

"SO WE'LL DO IT THE *HARD WAY*," HE SAID, AND PHARAMOND SUPPLIED A TRUCK.

A MIDNIGHT SKATER RUNNING BOOTLEG LIQUOR AND PORNOGRAPHY DOWN TO THE RESERVATIONS.

SOME *PILGRIMAGE*, RACHEL THOUGHT. SOME *SHAMAN*.

I DON'T HAVE TO DO THIS, YOU KNOW? I'M NO FUCKIN' *TOURIST* BUS. I GOT MY OWN WAYS OF WORKIN'. FUCKIN' FARRELL.

I OWE 'IM *MONEY*, NOT FUCKIN' *BLOOD*, OKAY? I GOT MY RIGHTS.

ARE YOU GONNA TELL ME WHERE WE'RE GOING?

I'VE *ALREADY* TOLD YOU. TSOODZIL, THE TURQUOISE MOUNTAIN, KNOWN IN THE MUNDANE WORLD AS MOUNT TAYLOR. YOUR PEOPLE'S MOST SACRED PLACE.

DON'T KEEP SAYING *MY* PEOPLE. ONLY MY DAD IS NAVAJO. IF I HAVE ANY PEOPLE THEY'RE IN L.A.

SO APART FROM BEING *SACRED*, WHAT ELSE HAS THIS PLACE GOT GOING FOR IT?

IT'S WHERE THE WORLD BEGAN.

THE WORLD BEGAN IN ALBUQUERQUE?

THIS COULD KICKSTART A WHOLE NEW RELIGION.

I NEED A FUCKING SMOKE. YOU PEOPLE TALK TOO MUCH. EXCUSE ME.

OKAY. I'M SORRY. BAD JOKE.

SO TELL ME ABOUT TSOODZIL.

IT'S NOT ABOUT TSOODZIL, GIRL. IT'S ABOUT *YOU*.

ME?

HUMANITY.

ALL THE RACES OF MAN TELL THE STORY OF THEIR OWN ORIGINS, BUT THEY ALL DISAGREE ON THE DETAILS.

DO THE DETAILS MATTER?

THE DETAILS ARE ALL THAT MATTERS.

THE BIBLE TELLS THAT STORY IN TERMS OF TIME--ONE THING AFTER ANOTHER. *FIRST* THERE WAS DARKNESS, *THEN* THERE WAS LIGHT.

YOUR PEOPLE REMEMBER IT DIFFERENTLY.

THEY SEE THE DARKNESS AS A TUNNEL THAT THEY CRAWLED THROUGH TO REACH THE LIGHT. A VERTICAL TUNNEL. THE LIGHT WAS IN ANOTHER PLACE, FAR ABOVE. THIS MEANS *NOTHING* TO YOU, DOES IT?

UMM...NOT A LOT. IS IT A BIRTH METAPHOR?

NO. IT'S THE THING FOR WHICH BIRTH *IS* A METAPHOR.

IN ANY CASE, THE *DINÉ* TELL THE STORY AS A JOURNEY. A HARD AND TERRIBLE JOURNEY. THE PLACE THEY STARTED FROM WAS FIRST WORLD.

WHERE THE DARKNESS WAS. WHERE IT STILL *IS*.

"UNDERSTAND ME. WHAT-EVER LIVED THERE THEN LIVES THERE STILL, THOUGH YOUR KIND ABANDONED THIS PLACE HALF A MILLION YEARS AGO. THERE ARE FORESTS OF BLACK OAKS, A HUNDRED FEET TALL, STANDING INVISIBLE IN THE DARK. THERE ARE CREATURES ...PREDATORS... THAT HAVE NOT EATEN IN GEOLOGICAL AGES."

"YOU HAVE FORGOTTEN THE VOICELESS, BUT THEY HAVE NOT FORGOTTEN YOU. THEY WANT YOU TO COME HOME. WANT THE FEEL OF YOUR FEAR AND YOUR WORSHIP. BUT WHILE THE DARKNESS IS A HOME FOR THEM, FOR YOU IT WAS ONLY A WOMB."

"YOU BETRAYED THEM WHEN YOU WERE BORN INTO THE LIGHT. AND I DON'T IMAGINE FOR A MOMENT THAT THEY'VE LEARNED TO LET GO."

KILLED A BIRD. WELCOME BACK.

MORNING-TOWN, KIDDIES. END OF THE FUCKIN' LINE.

WHAT... WHAT WAS THAT? WAS THERE A BUMP?

HAVE YERSELVES A NICE CAMP-OUT, EH?

AND GET 'ER BACK TO SCHOOL WHEN YOU'RE DONE WITH 'ER.

YOU WORK FOR PHARAMOND, SO YOU'RE NOT MINE TO CHASTISE.

ALL THE SAME, FOR YOUR LACK OF RESPECT SOME PUNISH-MENT IS DUE. SAY... THE PERMA-NENT LOSS OF SEXUAL POTENCY.

HEY! WHADDYA...? WHADDYA MEAN?

HEY, WAS THAT S'POSED TO BE FUNNY?

I AIN'T LAUGHING. YOU HEAR ME? BASTARD!

FARRELL

CAN WE... STOP... FOR... A REST?

WE'RE NEARLY THERE. YOU CAN REST AT THE TOP.

≷ HUFF ≷

FUNNY, IT DIDN'T LOOK SO *STEEP* FROM DOWN THERE.

IT WASN'T. THAT WAS MOUNT TAYLOR. *THIS* IS TSOODZIL.

YOU SAID MOUNT TAYLOR *IS* TSOODZIL. TWO NAMES FOR THE SAME THING.

THEN IMAGINE WE'RE CLIMBING THE *NAME* RATHER THAN THE *MOUNTAIN*, IF THAT MAKES IT ANY EASIER.

TRUTH IS A LOCAL PHENOMENON, LIKE A MICRO-CLIMATE.

WELL YOU KNOW, I FUCKING *HATE* BEING PATRONIZED AND I FUCKING *HATE* BEING USED, SO I'M JUST GONNA SIT HERE TILL I GET AN ANSWER I UNDERSTAND.

ALL RIGHT. YOU FELL ASLEEP. BUT BECAUSE OF YOUR FEELINGS OF GUILT OVER PAUL'S DEATH, IT'S A SHALLOW, RESTLESS SLEEP. YOU'RE DREAMING ME. YOU'RE DREAMING ALL OF THIS.

YEAH, THAT'S JUST ABOUT POSSIBLE. I THINK I WOULD'VE PUT IN A BOB'S BIG BOY HALFWAY UP, THOUGH.

PHARAMOND SAID WE COULD COME UP HERE BECAUSE I'M *NAVAJO*. IS THAT THE ONLY REASON YOU BROUGHT ME? BECAUSE YOU COULDN'T GET IN BY YOURSELF?

NO. NOT THE ONLY REASON. ARE YOU RESTED NOW?

IT SOUNDS PLAUSIBLE ENOUGH, IN THIS PLACE AND AT THIS TIME. SHE PLAYS WITH THE IDEA. A DREAM-RACHEL CARRYING OUT A DREAM-QUEST. A FIGURE OUT OF FANTASY TO GUARD AND SAVE HER...

DREAMS HAVE THEIR OWN LOGIC, OF COURSE, AND THEIR OWN AGENDAS.

WHOA.

WE'RE NOT GOING DOWN *THERE*...

ARE WE?

NOT YET. WE HAVE TO SPEAK TO BLUE FLINT GIRL FIRST. THIS IS WHERE SHE LIVES.

IS THAT BLUE FLINT GIRL'S *GRANDMA* OR WHAT?

IT'S JUST HER name--*ONE* OF HER NAMES. SHE'S OLDER THAN YOUR ENTIRE RACE.

COME ON. I'D LIKE TO GET THIS PART OVER WITH.

AH, YOU'RE HERE AT LAST. YOU MUST BE TIRED. SIT, AND EAT WITH ME.

ACTUALLY, MOTHER OF WHIRLWINDS, OUR BUSINESS IS FAIRLY PRESSING. WE'D LIKE TO GO STRAIGHT--

BE QUIET, ATSE'HASHKE. I WAS SPEAKING TO MY *GRAND-DAUGHTER.*

WHO? ME?

COME DOWN HERE, CHILD. SIT WITH ME ON THE GROUND. I WANT TO TALK TO YOU.

UMM. HI. HOW'S IT GOING?

NOT WELL. NOT WELL AT ALL. YOUR SPIRIT CRIES OUT LIKE AN *ANIMAL* IN A TRAP. IT HURTS ME TO SEE YOU IN SUCH PAIN.

YEAH, EVERYTHING'S PRETTY FUCKED UP RIGHT NOW. I DID SOMETHING TERRIBLE AND I'M...I'M TRYING TO MAKE IT OKAY AGAIN. LUCIFER'S HELPING ME.

I'VE COOKED CORN PANCAKES IN BEAR'S GREASE. EAT. THEY'LL GIVE YOU STRENGTH.

ATSE'HASHKE, I HAVEN'T MADE ENOUGH PANCAKES FOR YOU. GO FILL THE JUG WITH WATER AND I'LL MAKE SOME MORE.

YOU JUST LOVE TO TWIST THE KNIFE, DON'T YOU?

THEY'RE GOOD?

THEY'RE...THE WORST THING I'VE EVER TASTED IN MY WHOLE LIFE.

BUT STILL THEY'RE GOOD. EAT THEM ALL.

GRANDDAUGHTER, HE IS *NOT* HELPING YOU. BE SURE OF THAT. ATSE'-HASHKE HAS HIS OWN REASONS FOR EVERY-THING HE DOES.

BUT HE SAID IF I CAME WITH HIM I'D GET MY *BROTHER* BACK.

THAT IS NOT WHAT HE SAID. THE CRYING OF YOUR OWN SPIRIT MADE YOU DEAF TO HIS WORDS.

AND NOW HE HAS WALKED IN YOUR FOOTPRINTS TO THIS HOLY PLACE.

I WALKED IN *HIS* FOOTPRINTS, OKAY? HE GOT ME HERE, AND HE'S GIVING ME A CHANCE TO DO WHAT I NEED TO DO.

NO--WHAT *HE* NEEDS TO DO. BUT NO MATTER. YOU'LL REMEMBER THE WAY HERE ANOTHER TIME, AND YOU'LL BE WELCOME --IF YOU COME ALONE.

LOOK, I'M *STAYING* WITH HIM. HE PULLED ME OUT OF A LOT OF SHIT ALREADY.

CHRIST, MY *STOMACH!* THOSE WERE JUST CORN PANCAKES, RIGHT?

YES. BUT THE GREASE OF A BEAR GIVES *STRENGTH* TO THE HEART AND MIND. YOU WILL NEED THAT.

ONE JUG OF WATER. IF YOU'RE REALLY GOING TO MAKE ME *EAT* THOSE THINGS, GO LIGHT ON THE BEAR'S GREASE. VERY LIGHT.

TCH. THIS IS NO TIME TO SIT AND FILL YOUR STOMACH, ATSE'HASHKE, I THOUGHT YOU WERE IN A *HURRY.*

HERE, GRANDDAUGHTER. I HAVE A GIFT FOR YOU.

WHAT IS IT?

A JISH.

WHAT'S A JISH?

A MEDICINE POUCH. IT WILL TAKE YOU WHERE YOU HAVE TO GO, AND IT WILL BRING YOU BACK.

MOTHER OF WHIRLWINDS, I WAS *PROMISED* A GUIDE.

SO? AND NOW YOU HAVE ONE.

THIS GIRL? HOW CAN *SHE* GUIDE ME WHEN SHE DOESN'T KNOW THE WAY HERSELF? THIS IS ABSURD.

BUT THESE ARE STRANGE TIMES, ATSE'HASHKE--THE WISEST ARE LOST. AND YOUR LITTLE TRICK WITH THE KNIFE WILL ONLY TELL YOU WHEN YOU'VE ARRIVED. OPEN THE POUCH, CHILD.

I CAN'T UNTIE THE... OH YEAH. OKAY.

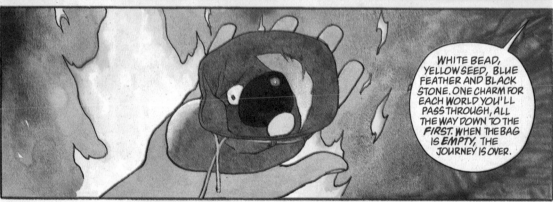

WHITE BEAD, YELLOW SEED, BLUE FEATHER AND BLACK STONE. ONE CHARM FOR EACH WORLD YOU'LL PASS THROUGH, ALL THE WAY DOWN TO THE *FIRST.* WHEN THE BAG IS *EMPTY,* THE JOURNEY IS OVER.

THANKS. THANK YOU. BUT... I MEAN... IS THIS GONNA *WORK?* AM I GONNA SEE PAUL AGAIN?

SOMETIMES THE TRUTH IS FALSER THAN ANY LIE. I CAN'T ANSWER THOSE QUESTIONS. WHEN THIS IS OVER, GO TO YOUR GRANDFATHER. ASK HIM TO SING A BLESSING WAY FOR YOU.

MY GRAND-FATHER? YOU *KNOW* HIM?

OH YES. I HAVE HAD TO DEAL WITH HOSTEEN SAM THREE TIMES. BUT YOU MUST GO NOW. WE'LL TALK AGAIN.

SA'AH NAAGHÁII BIK'EH HÓZHÓ, RACHEL.

AND WHILE YOU OPEN THE WAY FOR HIM, KEEP YOUR EYES AT YOUR BACK.

WORDS TO LIVE BY, RACHEL. I HOPE YOU'RE WRITING THEM DOWN.

THIS IS GETTING TOO WEIRD FOR ME. HOW COME SHE *KNOWS* ME? HOW COME SHE'S MET MY GRANDAD?

SHE KNOWS ALL THE DINER--EVEN THE HALF-BREEDS. AND A STRONG SHAMAN WILL SOMETIMES GET TO MEET HER FACE-TO-FACE.

AFTER YOU.

AFTER ME? YOU MEAN, I GO DOWN THERE *FIRST?*

YOU'RE MY GUIDE, AREN'T YOU?

UMM. YEAH, BUT I DON'T...

THEN GUIDE ME.

BUT I DON'T KNOW *SHIT* ABOUT THIS. IT'S NOT... I MEAN, NONE OF IT IS *REAL*, IS IT? THE REAL WORLD'S REAL. NORTH HOLLYWOOD IS REAL. THIS IS JUST..."CRAZY STUFF.

IT'S THE JOURNEY OF THE SPIRIT TO THE PLACE IT NEVER LEFT. WISE MEN SPEND MORE YEARS THAN YOU'VE *LIVED* PREPARING FOR IT.

BUT THERE YOU GO. THERE'S NEVER A WISE MAN AROUND WHEN YOU NEED ONE. YOU'LL JUST HAVE TO IMPROVISE.

OKAY. THEN I'M GONNA LEAVE THE WHITE BEAD RIGHT HERE IN THE MUD.

IT STANDS FOR ME, UP TO MY NECK IN SHIT AS USUAL.

THOSE LOOK LIKE FISH SKELETONS.

THEY *ARE* FISH SKELETONS.

THERE WAS A FLOOD HERE IN THE DAWN AGE THAT KILLED MANY OF YOUR PEOPLE.

PLEASE. KEEP YOUR EYES ON THE PATH.

RACHEL...

YOU STOLE MY BARBIE DREAM 'VETTE. YOU KNOW YOU DID.

EWWW!

RACHEL, YOU SHOULDN'T HAVE LAUGHED AT MY BRACE.

RACHEL, THIS IS YOUR MOTHER. WHY DO YOU NEVER WRITE TO ME, DARLING?

DON'T LEAVE ME, RACHEL.

WHY DID YOU KILL ME, RACHEL?

WHAT THE HELL IS *THIS*?

FOURTH WORLD. THE SALT WASTE LEFT BY THE FLOOD, WHERE NO SEED GROWS.

AS FOR THE FISH... THEY'RE SPEAKING TO YOU, NOT ME, SO I CAN'T COMMENT.

SO THEY'RE THE VOICES OF MY SUBCONSCIOUS *GUILT* OR SOMETHING, RIGHT?

PERHAPS. I'M NOT BIG ON PSYCHO-ANALYSIS.

IN WHICH CASE THEY CAN GO *SCREW* THEMSELVES. ENOUGH IS ENOUGH!

IF THIS IS A SPIRIT JOURNEY, EVERY-THING'S GONNA TURN OUT TO BE SOME HOKEY SYMBOL.

LIKE THIS IS A BARREN LAND WHERE SEEDS DON'T GROW...

...AND I JUST *HAPPEN* TO HAVE A SEED RIGHT HERE IN THE POUCH.

OKAY. THERE WE GO.

LET'S MAKE THE DESERT BLOOM, WHY DON'T WE?

PLISH!

CHRIST ON A BIKE!

WELL DONE. YOU'VE FOUND OUT WHERE THE FLOOD WATERS WENT.

AND I THINK YOU'VE SUCCEEDED IN ATTRACTING THEIR ATTENTION.

GREAT.

FUCKING PERFECT.

WHAT DO WE DO NOW?

WE WAIT. THIS WON'T TAKE LONG.

LUCIFER, I CAN'T SWIM. I'M GONNA DROWN!

NOT IF THE WATER IS ONLY SYMBOLIC.

OH FOR CHRIST'S SAKE! DON'T JUST STAND THERE TAKING CHEAP SHOTS, DO SOMETHING!

TRY *BREATHING.* YOU'LL BE AMAZED HOW MUCH MORE COMFORTABLE YOU'LL FIND IT.

IT'S BACK UP IN THE SKY, WHERE IT WAS. YOU SAVED US. YOU HIT THE REWIND BUTTON.

NO. IT ALLOWED US TO PASS THROUGH IT. WE'RE IN THIRD WORLD NOW, *BENEATH* THE FLOOD.

THERE'S A LOT OF STUFF THAT'S GOING OVER MY HEAD HERE.

YOU *ASTONISH* ME.

I MEAN, THIS PLACE IS SMACK IN THE MIDDLE OF THE *DESERT.* OUT IN THE REAL WORLD, I MEAN.

THE *REAL* WORLD?

YOU KNOW WHAT I MEAN. SO WHERE DID ALL THE WATER COME FROM? HOW COME THERE WAS A FLOOD?

THE *USUAL* REASONS-- THE EVIL OF THE PEOPLE MADE THE ELEMENTS MOVE FROM THEIR PROPER ORDER. BE CAREFUL HERE. THIRD WORLD IS STILL FULL OF THE RESIDUE OF THAT EVIL.

MAYBE IT'S TIME FOR SOME MORE MEDICINE MAN STUFF.

I'VE JUST GOT THE FEATHER AND THE STONE LEFT NOW. WHICH ONE D'YOU RECKON COMES NEXT? I'M THINKING MAYBE THE FEATHER...

BRING IT HERE, RACHEL. I'LL SHOW YOU WHAT TO DO.

HUH?

IT'S EASY. GIVE ME THE JISH AND I'LL SHOW YOU. I'LL TEACH YOU HOW TO BE A *SKINWALKER* AND CHANGE YOUR SHAPE.

PAUL! OH MY GOD! WHAT ARE YOU DOING HERE?

THIS IS CRAZY. YOU'RE *TALKING.* YOU'RE TALKING LIKE THERE WAS NEVER ANYTHING WRONG WITH YOU.

THERE'S STRONG MAGIC HERE. GIVE ME THE JISH.

YOU KNOW I NEVER WANTED TO HURT YOU, PAUL. IT WAS AN ACCIDENT. IT JUST...

NOW, WHORE, LET ME *SHOW* YOU WHAT HURT IS. LET ME TEACH YOU ALL THE WAYS OF IT.

UUUUH!

GET OFF ME! YOU'RE NOT PAUL! LET ME GO!

I AM THE GREAT STONE. IF YOU STRUGGLE IT WILL BE BETTER FOR ME, WORSE FOR YOU.

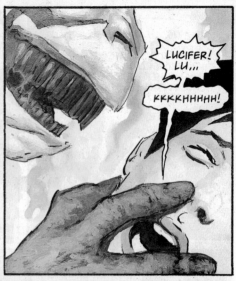

LUCIFER! LU...

KKKKHHHHH!

...?

BUT THE HOLY PEOPLE HAVE GONE. THERE'S NO POWER HERE GREAT ENOUGH TO...

NO! I WAS BORN FROM A WOMAN'S WOMB! I AM FLESH NOW, WARM FLESH! I WON'T...

I TOLD YOU TO BE CAREFUL.

YEAH. YEAH, YOU DID.

OH.

OH FUCK.

COME HERE. THERE'S SOMETHING I NEED TO SHOW YOU.

THIS GULF IS SECOND WORLD, AND AT THE BOTTOM IS FIRST WORLD.

WE CAN'T GO ANY FURTHER--UNLESS *YOU* CAN FIND US A WAY DOWN.

FINE. LET'S TRY THE MAGIC FEATHER. IT WORKED FOR *DUMBO.*

OKAY. WE CAME. WE SAW. WE ALMOST GOT RAPED BY A *ROCK.* NOW CAN WE...

WHOOOAAA!

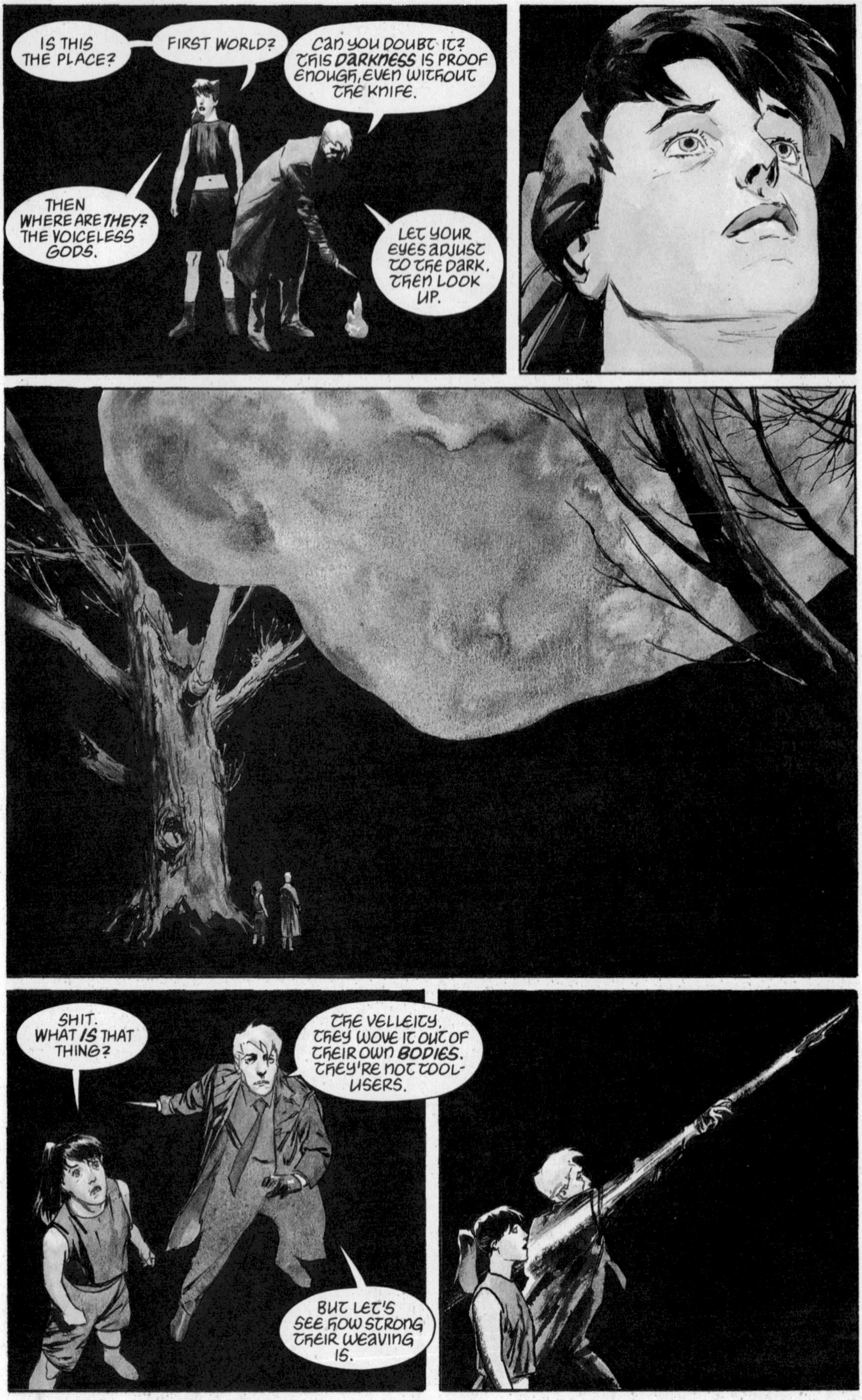
IS THIS THE PLACE?
FIRST WORLD?
CAN YOU DOUBT IT? THIS DARKNESS IS PROOF ENOUGH, EVEN WITHOUT THE KNIFE.
THEN WHERE ARE THEY? THE VOICELESS GODS.
LET YOUR EYES ADJUST TO THE DARK. THEN LOOK UP.
SHIT. WHAT IS THAT THING?
THE VELLEITY. THEY WOVE IT OUT OF THEIR OWN BODIES. THEY'RE NOT TOOL-USERS.
BUT LET'S SEE HOW STRONG THEIR WEAVING IS.

THEY STOPPED IT. WHAT NOW?

BE QUIET. IT'S STILL MOVING. MY WILL IS STRONGER THAN THEIRS.

SSSSSSSSSSS

SSSHRAKKK!

DID YOU THINK FIRE WOULD BURN ME?

I'M THE LIGHTBRINGER, THE SHEPHERD OF SUNS.

NOW UNTIE THAT KNOT--BECAUSE IF I HAVE TO DO IT MYSELF THERE'LL BE A CERTAIN AMOUNT OF COLLATERAL DAMAGE.

YOU CANNOT HURT US HERE IN OUR PLACE OF POWER. THE FAITH OF HUMANKIND IS GROUNDED THROUGH US. WE CAN MOVE MOUNTAINS NOW.

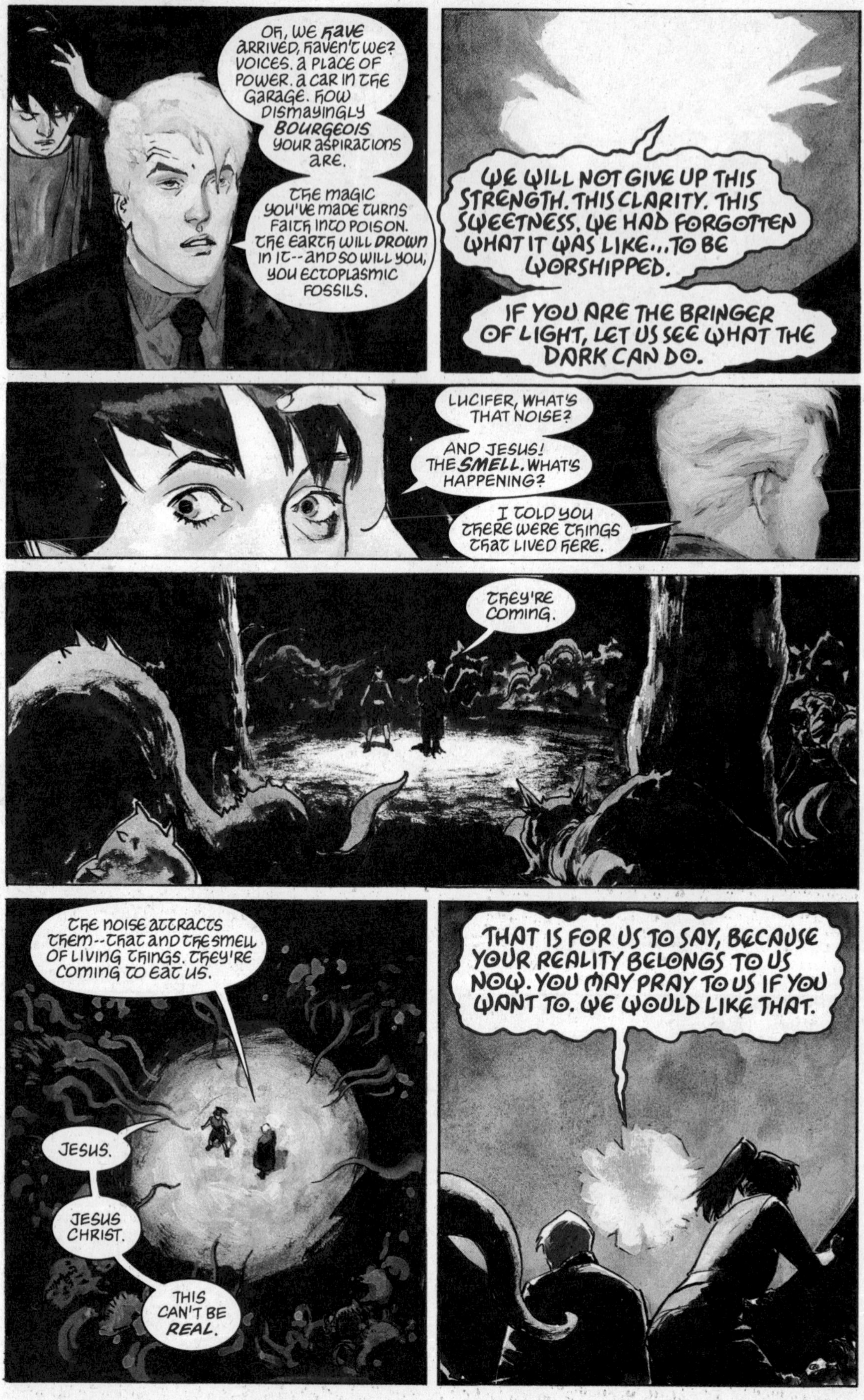
OH, WE HAVE ARRIVED, HAVEN'T WE? VOICES. A PLACE OF POWER. A CAR IN THE GARAGE. HOW DISMAYINGLY BOURGEOIS YOUR ASPIRATIONS ARE.
THE MAGIC YOU'VE MADE TURNS FAITH INTO POISON. THE EARTH WILL DROWN IN IT--AND SO WILL YOU, YOU ECTOPLASMIC FOSSILS.
WE WILL NOT GIVE UP THIS STRENGTH. THIS CLARITY. THIS SWEETNESS. WE HAD FORGOTTEN WHAT IT WAS LIKE...TO BE WORSHIPPED.
IF YOU ARE THE BRINGER OF LIGHT, LET US SEE WHAT THE DARK CAN DO.
LUCIFER, WHAT'S THAT NOISE?
AND JESUS! THE SMELL. WHAT'S HAPPENING?
I TOLD YOU THERE WERE THINGS THAT LIVED HERE.
THEY'RE COMING.
THE NOISE ATTRACTS THEM--THAT AND THE SMELL OF LIVING THINGS. THEY'RE COMING TO EAT US.
JESUS.
JESUS CHRIST.
THIS CAN'T BE REAL.
THAT IS FOR US TO SAY, BECAUSE YOUR REALITY BELONGS TO US NOW. YOU MAY PRAY TO US IF YOU WANT TO. WE WOULD LIKE THAT.

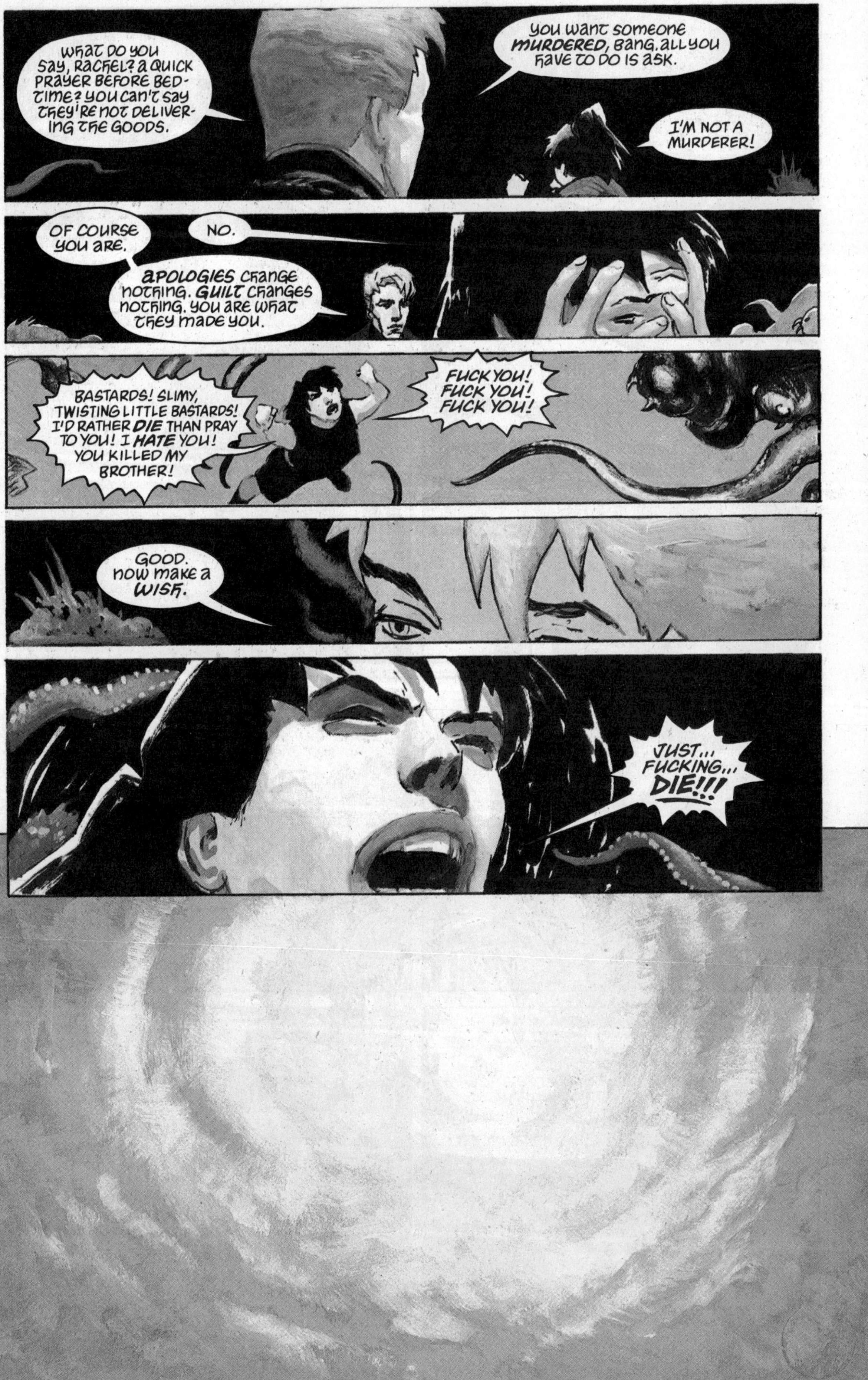
WHAT DO YOU SAY, RACHEL? A QUICK PRAYER BEFORE BED-TIME? YOU CAN'T SAY THEY'RE NOT DELIVER-ING THE GOODS.
YOU WANT SOMEONE MURDERED, BANG. ALL YOU HAVE TO DO IS ASK.
I'M NOT A MURDERER!
OF COURSE YOU ARE.
NO.
APOLOGIES CHANGE NOTHING. GUILT CHANGES NOTHING. YOU ARE WHAT THEY MADE YOU.
BASTARDS! SLIMY, TWISTING LITTLE BASTARDS! I'D RATHER DIE THAN PRAY TO YOU! I HATE YOU! YOU KILLED MY BROTHER!
FUCK YOU! FUCK YOU! FUCK YOU!
GOOD. NOW MAKE A WISH.
JUST... FUCKING... DIE!!!

THAT'S THAT, I THINK. TIME TO GO HOME.

I....I DON'T GET IT. WHERE DID THEY GO? WHAT HAPPENED?

YOU HAPPENED.

THE VELLEITY WAS DESIGNED TO SATISFY DESIRE. IT'S A COMMODITY I'M SHORT ON, BUT YOURS DID WELL ENOUGH.

WHEN YOU WISHED IT GONE, IT HAD NO CHOICE BUT TO DESTROY ITSELF. BY THE WAY, YOU'LL BE NEEDING THIS.

WAIT. WAIT A MINUTE. THAT WAS THE THING THAT WAS GRANTING WISHES, RIGHT?

AND NOW IT'S GONE. SO HOW DO I GET PAUL BACK?

YOU DON'T. IT'S TOO LATE NOW.

BUT YOU....YOU SAID...

I SAID I'D GIVE YOU AN OPPORTUNITY.

NOT STEP-BY-STEP INSTRUCTIONS.

YOU TRICKED ME! YOU LIED TO ME!

PERHAPS. BUT IF YOU REALLY WANTED HIM BACK, IT WOULD HAVE HAPPENED.

I SUSPECT THAT WHAT YOU ACTUALLY WANTED WAS AN EXCUSE TO FORGIVE YOURSELF.

I'VE STILL GOT THE JISH, LUCIFER. I'M NOT TAKING YOU BACK WITH ME. I'M GOING TO LEAVE YOU HERE TO ROT, YOU BASTARD!

YES, I THOUGHT WE MIGHT GET TO THAT.

I SAID YOU NEEDED IT, NOT ME. NOW THAT THE WEATHER'S CLEARED, I THINK I'LL JUST WALK.

IN ANY CASE, YOU SHOULD BE GRATEFUL THAT YOU'RE LEAVING HERE IN ONE PIECE. I SAVED YOUR LIFE AND YOUR MAIDENHEAD AND I CONSIDER US WELL QUIT.

CONSUMMATUM EST.

I'LL FIND YOU SOMEDAY. I WILL, I MEAN IT. WHEN I'M STRONG ENOUGH TO TAKE YOU ON.

THAT'S A PITY. YOU'D MANAGED TO KEEP YOUR HEAD UP ABOVE THE MELO-DRAMA UNTIL NOW.

GOODBYE, RACHEL.

"The general opinion is that you did well, Lucifer Morningstar."

"It's not an opinion that I share."

This is what you asked for, I believe.

Thank you, Amenadiel. Grudging praise is the most flattering of all.

And the girl?

You took advantage of her innocence and her grief. You have *damaged* her. You may even have destroyed her.

There's a whole shelfload of Christian commentaries about how good suffering is for the soul. Have you read them? They're great fun.

I don't think I'd have the stomach for them right now.

You fired me, Amenadiel. You gave me free rein and total absolution.

I carried out my...

Yes, of course you did. Now off you go and wash your hands--

--I suggest steel wool.

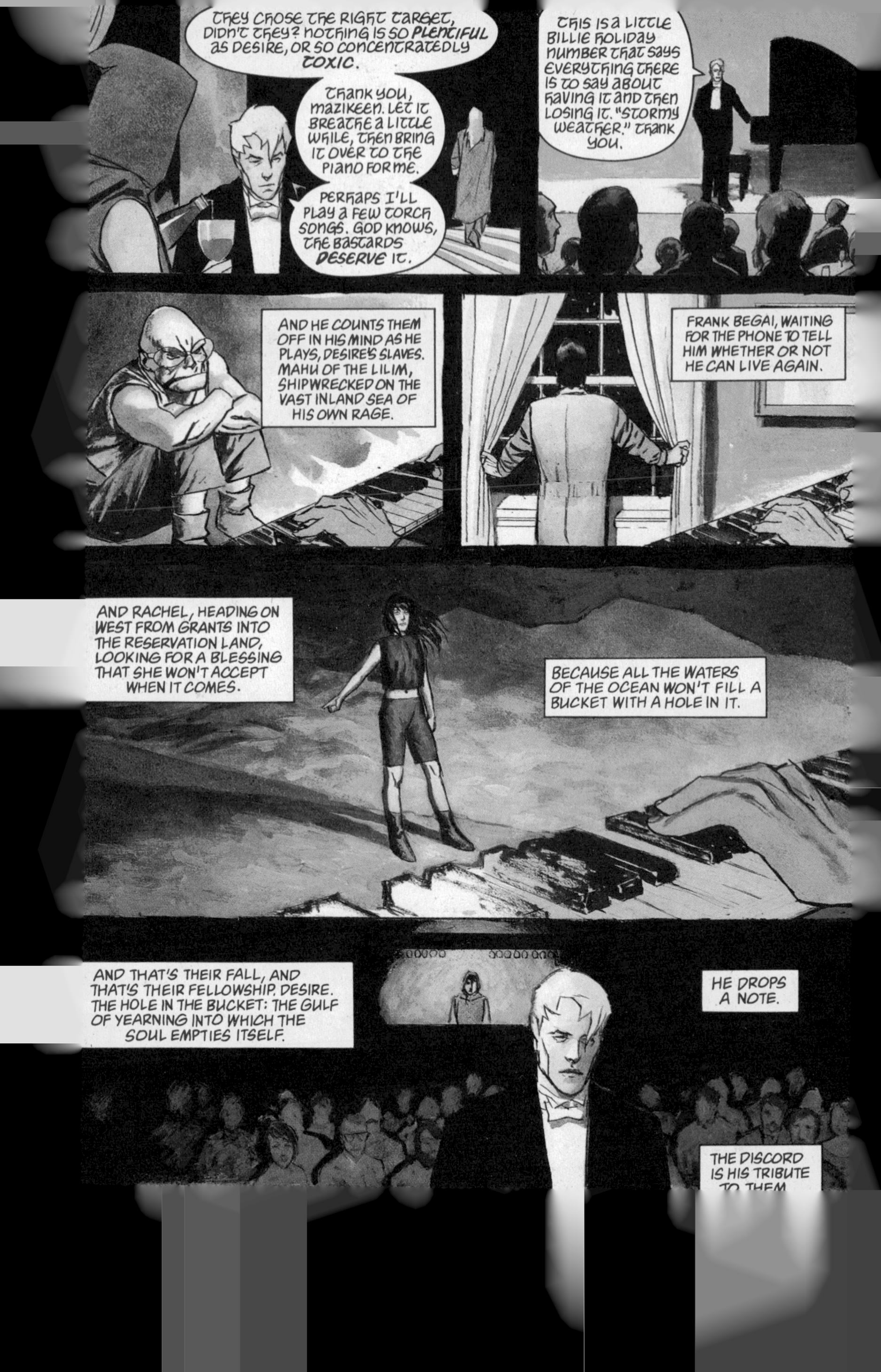
THEY CHOSE THE RIGHT TARGET, DIDN'T THEY? NOTHING IS SO PLENTIFUL AS DESIRE, OR SO CONCENTRATEDLY TOXIC.
THANK YOU, MAZIKEEN. LET IT BREATHE A LITTLE WHILE, THEN BRING IT OVER TO THE PIANO FOR ME.
PERHAPS I'LL PLAY A FEW TORCH SONGS. GOD KNOWS, THE BASTARDS DESERVE IT.
THIS IS A LITTLE BILLIE HOLIDAY NUMBER THAT SAYS EVERYTHING THERE IS TO SAY ABOUT HAVING IT AND THEN LOSING IT. "STORMY WEATHER." THANK YOU.
AND HE COUNTS THEM OFF IN HIS MIND AS HE PLAYS, DESIRE'S SLAVES. MAHU OF THE LILIM, SHIPWRECKED ON THE VAST INLAND SEA OF HIS OWN RAGE.
FRANK BEGAI, WAITING FOR THE PHONE TO TELL HIM WHETHER OR NOT HE CAN LIVE AGAIN.
AND RACHEL, HEADING ON WEST FROM GRANTS INTO THE RESERVATION LAND, LOOKING FOR A BLESSING THAT SHE WON'T ACCEPT WHEN IT COMES.
BECAUSE ALL THE WATERS OF THE OCEAN WON'T FILL A BUCKET WITH A HOLE IN IT.
AND THAT'S THEIR FALL, AND THAT'S THEIR FELLOWSHIP. DESIRE. THE HOLE IN THE BUCKET: THE GULF OF YEARNING INTO WHICH THE SOUL EMPTIES ITSELF.
HE DROPS A NOTE.
THE DISCORD IS HIS TRIBUTE TO THEM

Divine Susano, son of Izanami, Speaker in Thunder...

Welcome, my Lord. Welcome to Hell.

YOUR KINDNESS IS MORE THAN MY WORTH, REMIEL OF THE SERAPHIM. THINGS HAVE *CHANGED* SINCE MY LAST VISIT.

YOUR OWN WORK ENTIRELY? OR DO YOU CONSULT WITH LORD LUCIFER FROM TIME TO TIME?

Never.

AH! FORGIVE MY IMPERTINENCE AND INCOMPREHENSION. I HAD HEARD THAT THE STAR OF MORNING HAD MADE HIS PEACE WITH HEAVEN.

No, no! There was a specific and discreet arrangement. He... did the Host a favor and was duly paid for it.

As for Lucifer's advice...

...Duma and I have done very well without it.

A SIX-CARD SPREAD

MIKE CAREY·WRITER   CHRIS WESTON·PENCILLER&
INKER PAGES 1, 2, 3 & 22   JAMES HODGKINS·INKER
PAGES 4-21   DANIEL VOZZO·COLORIST & SEPARATOR
ELLIE DE VILLE·LETTERER   DUNCAN FEGREDO·COVER
ARTIST   WILL DENNIS·ASSISTANT EDITOR   SHELLY
ROEBERG·EDITOR   SANDMAN CHARACTERS
CREATED BY GAIMAN, KIETH & DRINGENBERG

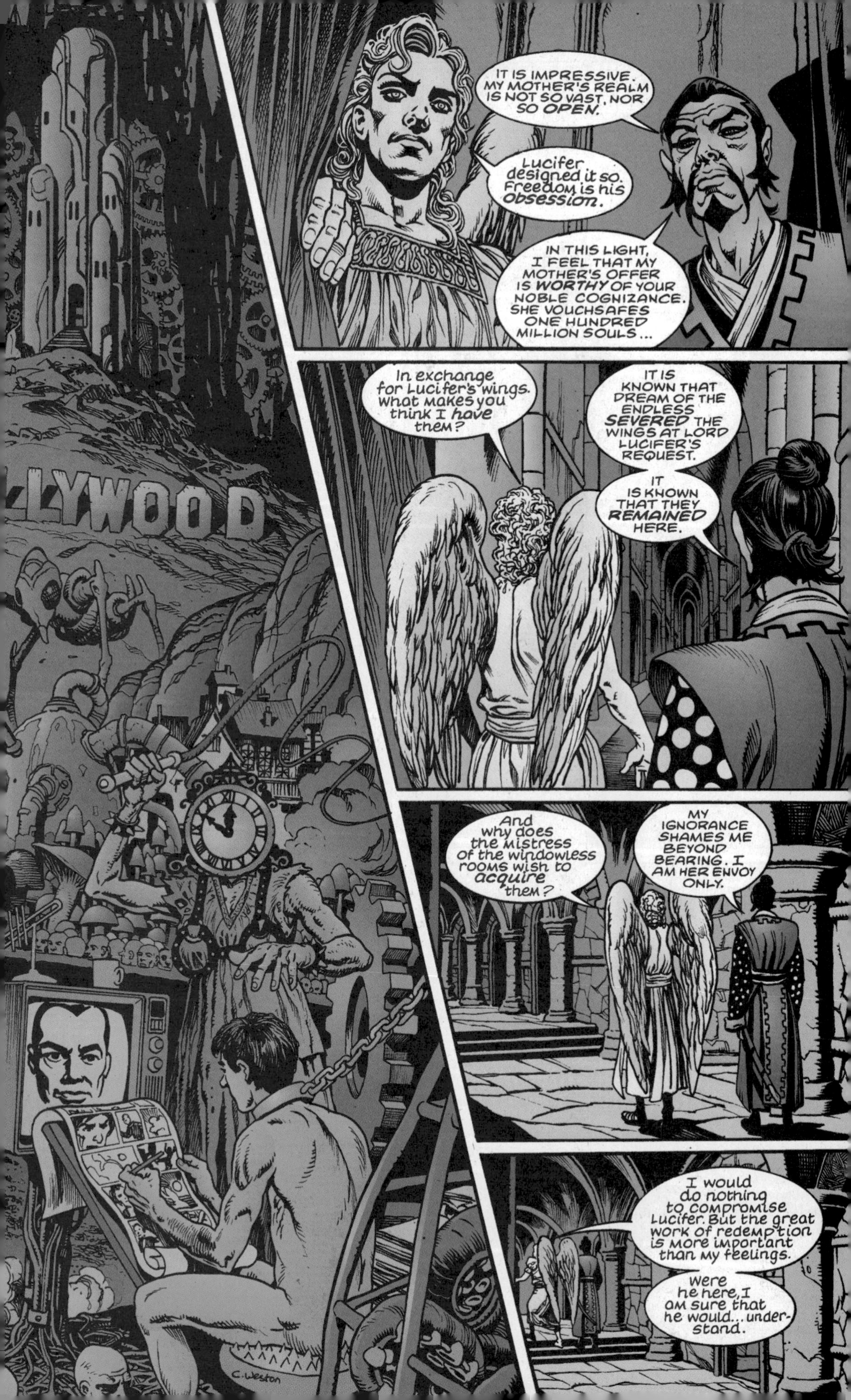
IT IS IMPRESSIVE. MY MOTHER'S REALM IS NOT SO VAST, NOR SO OPEN.
Lucifer designed it so. Freedom is his obsession.
IN THIS LIGHT, I FEEL THAT MY MOTHER'S OFFER IS WORTHY OF YOUR NOBLE COGNIZANCE. SHE VOUCHSAFES ONE HUNDRED MILLION SOULS...
In exchange for Lucifer's wings. What makes you think I have them?
IT IS KNOWN THAT DREAM OF THE ENDLESS SEVERED THE WINGS AT LORD LUCIFER'S REQUEST.
IT IS KNOWN THAT THEY REMAINED HERE.
And why does the mistress of the windowless rooms wish to acquire them?
MY IGNORANCE SHAMES ME BEYOND BEARING. I AM HER ENVOY ONLY.
I would do nothing to compromise Lucifer. But the great work of redemption is more important than my feelings.
Were he here, I am sure that he would... understand.
LLYWOOD
C. Weston

He is no longer the **lord of hell.** He is no longer the **agent of heaven.** Even his name Lucifer, the Lightbringer, describes a function from which he has resigned.

He has escaped from Providence. He has breakfasted on omelette and sliced pastourma. And now he folds the letter--

NOTHING WILL COME OF NOTHING.

--which is so searingly **blank** it seems to leave a hole in the air where it was.

HEOU SZHKOKE, NGY RROAHD?

ONLY TO MYSELF, MAZIKEEN.

I'M ONE MOVE AWAY FROM **ENDGAME.** I WAS JUST REVIEWING MY OPTIONS.

NGY RROAHD... IGH I CAN AKHHH, RHY HHKAVV RE HKONGH HHERE?

WHY? BECAUSE IN ANY DEALINGS WITH **HEAVEN** I'M INCLINED TO **DISSECT** THE GIFT HORSE AND HAVE A GOOD LOOK AT ITS GUTS.

I DON'T **TRUST** THE OLD BASTARD AS FAR AS I CAN **THROW** HIM.

TO RID HIMSELF OF A MINOR NUISANCE, HE GAVE ME AN OBJECT OF **INCONCEIVABLE** POWER.

THE LETTER **SEEMS** GENUINE. BUT IF IT WERE ME, I'D HAVE MADE SURE IT COULD NEVER BE **USED.**

SO I THOUGHT I'D COME TO HAMBURG, PULL MELEOS OUT FROM UNDER HIS **ROCK...**

...AND ASK HIM, VERY **POLITELY,** FOR A SIX-CARD SPREAD.

MUSIC — **DER TASCHENTURM**

MR. WEISS, WHAT SHOULD I DO WITH THE STUFF THAT CAME FROM ZWEMMERS?

DO YOU WANT ME TO...?

HE'S DISTRACTED. HE HAS BEEN FOR MOST OF THE DAY.

DISTURBED. THROWN OUT. NOT BY THE CRACKED SPINE OF THIS ORLANDO FURIOSO. A CRACKED SPINE CAN BE MENDED WITH PASTE AND STAIN.

IF ONLY ALL HIS PROBLEMS WERE SO TRACTABLE.

I'M SORRY, KARL. THE ZWEMMER BOOKS. YES. COULD YOU CHECK THEM AGAINST THE INVOICE?

THEN PUT THEM STRAIGHT ON THE SHELVES.

YES, MR. WEISS.

THE WOLF AND THE MAN IN MODERN HISTORY ARE DEVOURING EACH OTHER: TAKING TURNS TO BITE INTO FUR AND FLESH, TO SHIFT, GRIP AND TEAR, TO CHEW AND SWALLOW.

HE'S COMING, MELEOS.

THE BLIND WOMAN HOLDS A WHIP, WHOSE NINE HOOKED TAILS ARE STUCK TOGETHER WITH CONGEALING BLOOD. SHE IS SO TIRED FROM HER EXERTIONS THAT SHE HAS LOWERED HER SCALES.

HE IS HUNTING FOR TRUTH. HE WANTS TO CRACK IT BETWEEN HIS TEETH, AND SUCK ITS JUICE AND SPIT OUT ITS GRISTLE.

THE BASANOS REVEALS ITSELF ONLY TO THOSE IT WISHES TO ADDRESS, SO MELEOS SPEAKS IN A MURMUR, HIS LIPS BARELY MOVING.

VERY WELL. SO HE'S COMING. SHOULD I RUN AND HIDE?

DO YOU THINK I'M AFRAID OF LUCIFER?

WHY NOT? YOU'RE AFRAID OF *US*. SO AFRAID YOU KEEP US *BOUND* IN A BOX OF OAK AND IRON.

I'M *NOT* AFRAID OF YOU.

THEN LET US OUT TO *PLAY*. AND FLY. AND FUCK. AND *FEED*.

ALL THE THINGS YOU NEVER GET AROUND TO *YOUR-SELF* ANYMORE.

HI, KARL. WHERE'S *MR. WEISS?* I BROUGHT BACK THE *BOOK* HE LENT ME.

HE'S IN THE BACK. *TALKING* TO HIMSELF. *AGAIN.*

SO HOW'S LIFE? YOU'RE GETTING SOME NEW STOCK IN, YEAH?

NO, I'M MOVING *OLD* STOCK AROUND SO IT STAYS *FRESH*.

HEH. RIGHT.

YOUR LITTLE *PROTÉGÉ*, *MELEOS PHILOSOPHIA*, EH? THE *PURE* LOVE OF WISDOM.

CYNICISM IS EASY.

THANKS FOR THE LOAN, MR. WEISS. I REALLY *ENJOYED* THIS.

YOU'RE WELCOME, JAYESH. I HAVE MARCUSE'S *CRITIQUE* OF FREUD IF YOU'RE INTERESTED.

WELL... I DON'T KNOW. IT'S TOUGH STUFF. I'M NOT SURE I'M UP TO IT.

"A MAN GAINS HIS FIRST MEASURE OF WISDOM WHEN HE ADMITS HIS *IGNORANCE*."

BUT YOU TOOK *THAT* STEP A LONG TIME AGO, JAYESH. IT'S TIME TO HAVE SOME FAITH IN YOURSELF.

YEAH, WELL, YOU KNOW HOW IT IS.

I GET DISTRACTED TOO EASILY.

IT'S ALL ACADEMIC, ANYWAY. THERE'S NO WAY MY DAD IS GOING TO LET ME GO TO UNIVERSITY.

YOU'LL NEED TO *REASSURE* HIM, NOT...CONFRONT HIM.

HE HAS HIS *OWN* AMBITIONS FOR YOU. THAT'S ONLY HUMAN NATURE.

THIS IS HUMAN NATURE, MELEOS. TO SACRIFICE THE OTHER ON THE *ALTAR OF SELF.*

TAKE A LOOK AT MARCUSE ANYWAY, AND WE'LL TALK TOMORROW. I'M AFRAID I HAVE TO CLOSE UP NOW.

I'M EXPECTING *VISITORS.*

OH. OKAY. THANKS.

'BYE, KARL. SEE YOU LATER.

YEAH. I'M SURE OF IT.

THIS WILL KEEP UNTIL TOMORROW. TAKE THE POST AND THEN GO ON *HOME.*

VERY WELL, MR. WEISS.

NOW THAT'S SO MUCH MORE *COSY,* DON'T YOU THINK?

ES TUT MIR LEID WIR SIND GESCHLOSSEN: SIE MÜSSEN DIE GELBEN SEITEN LESSEN.

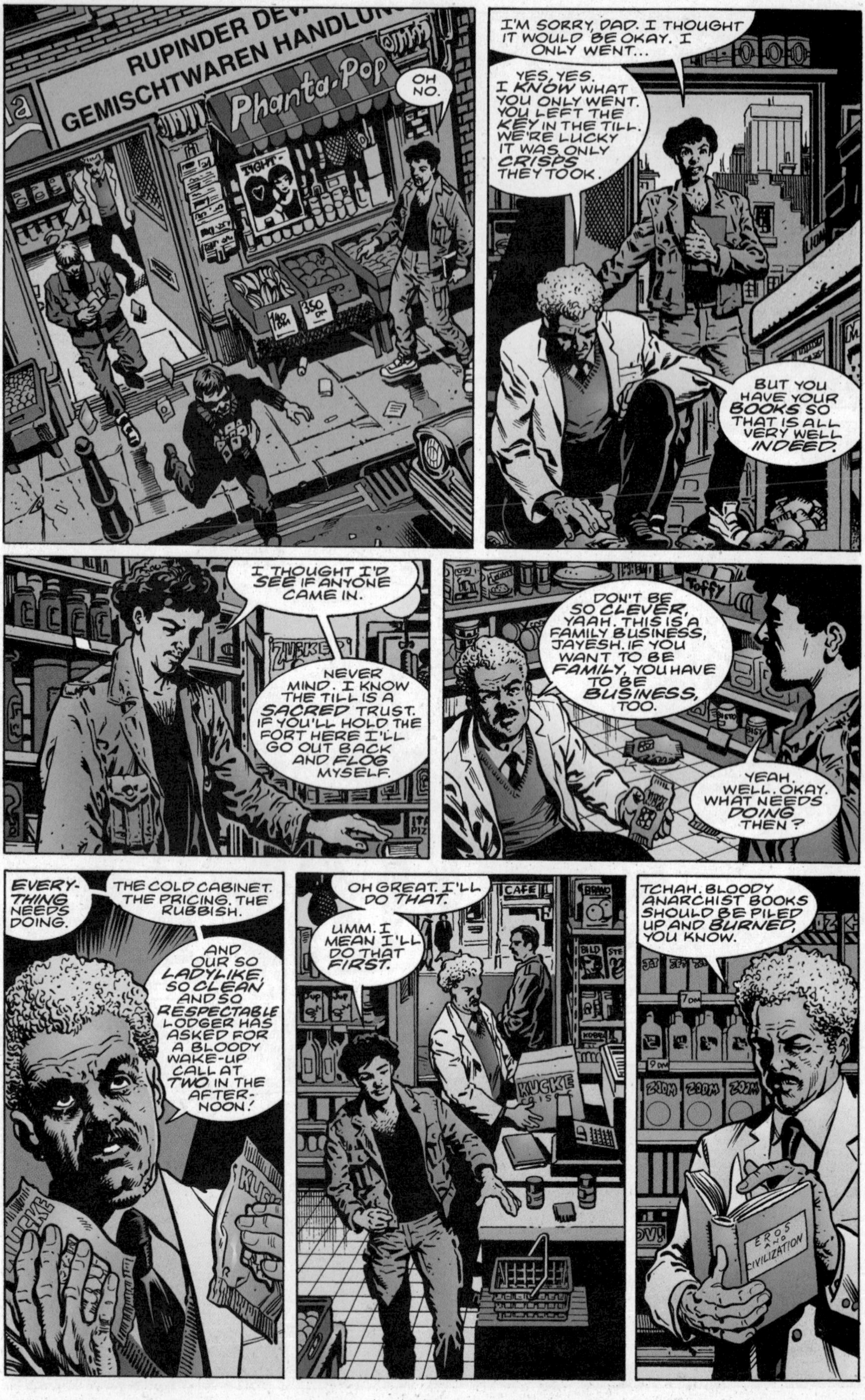
RUPINDER
GEMISCHTWAREN
Phanta-Pop
OH NO.
I'M SORRY, DAD. I THOUGHT IT WOULD BE OKAY. I ONLY WENT...
YES, YES. I KNOW WHAT YOU ONLY WENT. YOU LEFT THE KEY IN THE TILL. WE'RE LUCKY IT WAS ONLY CRISPS THEY TOOK.
BUT YOU HAVE YOUR BOOKS SO THAT IS ALL VERY WELL INDEED.
I THOUGHT I'D SEE IF ANYONE CAME IN.
NEVER MIND. I KNOW THE TILL IS A SACRED TRUST. IF YOU'LL HOLD THE FORT HERE I'LL GO OUT BACK AND FLOG MYSELF.
DON'T BE SO CLEVER, YAAH. THIS IS A FAMILY BUSINESS, JAYESH. IF YOU WANT TO BE FAMILY, YOU HAVE TO BE BUSINESS, TOO.
YEAH. WELL. OKAY. WHAT NEEDS DOING THEN?
EVERYTHING NEEDS DOING.
THE COLD CABINET. THE PRICING. THE RUBBISH.
AND OUR SO LADYLIKE, SO CLEAN AND SO RESPECTABLE LODGER HAS ASKED FOR A BLOODY WAKE-UP CALL AT TWO IN THE AFTERNOON!
OH GREAT. I'LL DO THAT.
UMM. I MEAN I'LL DO THAT FIRST.
TCHAH. BLOODY ANARCHIST BOOKS SHOULD BE PILED UP AND BURNED, YOU KNOW.
EROS AND CIVILIZATION

JILL? ARE YOU AWAKE? IT'S TEN PAST TWO.

KNK

I'VE BROUGHT YOU SOME COFFEE. I'LL JUST LEAVE IT HERE, SHOULD I?

HI, JAY. NAH, BRING IT IN. I'M *UP* ALREADY.

I DON'T SUPPOSE YOU BROUGHT A COUPLE OF YOUR MUM'S *SAMOSAS* TOO, BY ANY CHANCE?

YEAH, AND A BIT OF BRINJAL *PICKLE* IF YOU WANT.

COOL.

HUGO MERVEILLE AND JILL PRESTO

THE NEEDLE'S EYE

ZIRKUSWEG HAMBURG

GOD, THIS STUFF IS LIKE *ANGELS* STABBING YOUR TONGUE TO DEATH. I HAD TO *SKIP* SUPPER AGAIN.

HUGO HAD ME PRACTICING.

I LIKE THE EYELINER.

THANKS.

YOU WEAR A *PADDED* BRA? WHY WOULD YOU NEED TO DO THAT?

WHY ELSE? BECAUSE LOTS OF GUYS HAVE A *TIT* FIXATION. MOSTLY THEY DON'T EVEN LOOK YOU IN THE EYE UNTIL THEY'VE CHECKED OUT HOW YOU'RE *BUILT.*

BUT YOU ... I MEAN YOU'VE GOT A *PERFECT* FIGURE.

THANKS, JAY. I'M TOUCHED. I MEAN, YOU'RE AS *BENT* AS ...

...BUT I GUESS IT'S THE *THOUGHT* THAT COUNTS.

SPEAKING OF WHICH, DID YOU TRY THE *PISTOLKAMMER* YET?

OH JESUS, NO. I'M ALLOWED TO BE QUEER AND STILL HAVE *TASTE*, AREN'T I? THAT PRICKS-ON-PARADE STUFF IS JUST *EMBARRASSING*.

THEN DID YOU ASK *KARL* OUT?

I *ALMOST* DID, BUT I CHICKENED OUT. I MEAN, WHAT IF HE SAYS *NO*?

HE JUST *WORKS* TWO DOORS AWAY. AND I'M IN AND OUT OF THE SHOP ALL THE TIME. IT COULD GET PRETTY *UNCOMFORTABLE*.

ISN'T WALKING AROUND WITH A PERMANENT HARD-ON PRETTY UNCOMFORTABLE TOO?

I MEAN, I DON'T HAVE A *DICK* SO THIS ISN'T A VALID COMPARISON, BUT WHEN I'M *HORNY* I TEND TO...

I DON'T KNOW WHY I EVER *CONFIDED* IN YOU. YOU'RE A FOUL-MOUTHED *TART* WITH *SMALL TITS*. I MEAN, LET'S FACE IT...

GUILTY AS CHARGED. COME ON, JAY--PUT UP OR SHUT UP. YOU'VE BEEN MOONING AFTER HIM FOR THREE *MONTHS* NOW.

"...ANYONE WHO CAN'T GET *LAID* IN ST PAULI *ISN'T TRYING*."

HEY, HEY, MISTER. YOU WANT SOMETHING A BIT *FRESHER*?

GUCK MAL!

NO. THANK YOU. YOU HAVE NOTHING THAT I WANT.

YOU DON'T KNOW TILL YOU'VE *TRIED*. COME ON, MISTER. WHEN DID YOU LAST GET YOUR *PIPE* CLEANED?

GO *HOME* NOW, SIGRID MAHLER, AND YOU MAY BE IN TIME FOR YOUR *FATHER'S* FUNERAL.

WH...WHAT?

Oh. Oh god.

Papa.

Oh god forgive me.

ANG HHKISZ ISZ RHRERE RHRE RRIGSZ? HHKE ISZ ANG *ANKHYELH*.

HE'S A HISTORIAN. HE LIVES AMONG HUMANS IN ORDER TO CHRONICLE THEM.

ALTHOUGH PERHAPS IT'S ALSO A DECLARATION OF NEUTRALITY.

THIS WILL BE *EASIER* IF WE'RE NOT INTERRUPTED, MAZIKEEN. IF ANY *BIBLIOPHILES* SHOULD PASS THIS WAY, PERSUADE THEM TO KEEP ON GOING.

YESZ, NGY RROAHD.

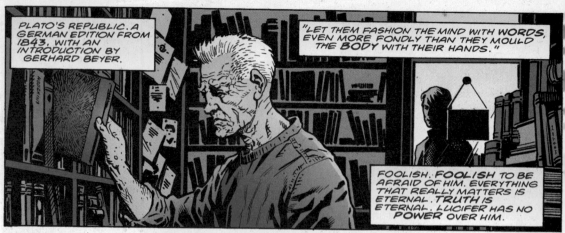

PLATO'S REPUBLIC. A GERMAN EDITION FROM 1843, WITH AN INTRODUCTION BY GERHARD BEYER.

"LET THEM FASHION THE MIND WITH *WORDS*, EVEN MORE FONDLY THAN THEY MOULD THE *BODY* WITH THEIR HANDS."

FOOLISH. FOOLISH TO BE AFRAID OF HIM. EVERYTHING THAT REALLY MATTERS IS ETERNAL. *TRUTH IS ETERNAL.* LUCIFER HAS NO *POWER* OVER HIM.

OH, MELEOS, YOU HAVE NO IDEA AT ALL HOW DEEP A *SILENCE* IS ABOUT TO FALL ON YOU.

BE QUIET.

NOTHING IS ETERNAL, MELEOS. EVEN THE SILVER CITY WILL *END.* SO HOW SHOULD THE SOUL OF *MAN* ENDURE?

I SAID BE *QUIET!* YOU'RE NOT EVEN HERE! YOU'RE *BURIED!*

BURIED SO DEEP THAT NO ONE WILL *EVER* FIND YOU!

TING. TING

GOOD AFTERNOON, LUCIFER. WAS IT SOMETHING *SPECIFIC* YOU WERE LOOKING FOR, OR WOULD YOU LIKE TO *BROWSE?*

HELLO, MELEOS. NO, THANK YOU.

I'M NOT LOOKING FOR A *BOOK.*

POLITIK

HESSE

TO TELL YOU THE TRUTH, I'M MORE IN THE MOOD FOR A *GAME* OF *CARDS.*

YOU MIND IF I SCRUMP A *PEPPERONI* THING, RUPINDER?

THEY ARE 80 PFENNIGS. YOU CAN *PAY* ME WHEN YOU PAY YOUR RENT.

COOL. I GOT A STUFFED OLIVE, TOO.

OUCH!

OW. SHIT. SORRY.

HEY. SIE SIND SCHAUS-PIELERIN, YEAH? A *PERFORM-ER?*

COOL MASK. WHERE ARE YOU PLAYING?

SEE, I'M IN CABARET MYSELF. A *MAGIC* ACT. HENCE THE HAND-CUFFS. I'M NOT INTO *BDSM* OR ANYTHING.

ALTHOUGH I DON'T SEE ANYTHING *WRONG* WITH SMACKING A GUY AROUND IF HE'S *UP* FOR IT, YOU KNOW?

LOOK. THIS GETS YOU AND A *FRIEND* IN WITH A 10 MARK DISCOUNT.

Hugo Merveille & Jill Presto

AT THE NEEDLE'S EYE CABARET ZIRKSWEG, HAMBURG TEL. HAMBURG 732 4964 HTTP://...OLE.NET

SATISFACTION GUARANTEED. HUGO'S A SHIT BUT HE GIVES GOOD MAGIC.

SEE YOU, YEAH?

I WOULD HAVE THOUGHT THIS SHOP WAS A LITTLE *SMALL* FOR YOUR NEEDS.

OR ARE YOU A *FRANCHISE* OPERATION NOW?

YOU CARE NOTHING ABOUT MY COLLECTION, LUCIFER. THERE'S NO NEED TO PRETEND.

ON THE CONTRARY, THERE'S SOMETHING QUEASILY *FASCINATING* ABOUT YOUR COLLECTION.

EVERY *INANE* SPECULATION THE HUMAN SPECIES HAS MADE ABOUT ITS ORIGINS. EVERY PERVERSE *CODE* BY WHICH THEY'VE EVER TRIED TO LIVE. EVERY HAM-FISTED HYMN.

I DON'T THINK ANYONE HAS *TRIED* BEFORE TO SCALE THE FORTRESS OF TRUTH BY BUILDING A SEIGE TOWER OF *BANALITIES*.

YOU! *YOU* TALK ABOUT TRUTH! YOU RECOGNIZE *NONE* EXCEPT THAT OF YOUR OWN WILL...

PERHAPS NOT. BUT AT LEAST THAT MAKES ME *CONSISTENT.*

I MEAN, YOU ALWAYS KNOW WHERE YOU *ARE* WITH ME.

AND WHERE YOU *ARE*, MELEOS, IS ON THE BRINK OF THE ABYSS, ABOUT TO DO A TRIPLE *BACK-FLIP* OVER THE EDGE.

I...I DON'T...

ONE *WORD* WILL DO IT.

I NEED TO CARRY OUT A *DIVINATION.*

WHICH MEANS THAT I NEED THE *DECK* YOU'VE CREATED.

THE BASANOS? HAH. YOU'LL FORGIVE ME IF I DON'T BELIEVE YOU.

WHAT WOULD YOU ASK IT? YOU'VE NEVER KNOWN THE FEELING OF DOUBT. YOU'VE NEVER NEEDED A BLESSING OR AN ABSOLUTION FOR ANYTHING YOU DID.

EVEN WHEN YOU PLUNGED US ALL INTO WAR.

I MAKE MY OWN CHOICES. AS YOU'VE DONE. AS EVERYONE DOES.

I'M LOOKING FOR INFORMATION, NOT A BLESSING.

DO YOU SEE THIS?

IT'S A LETTER OF PASSAGE. AND IT BEARS GOD'S IMPRIMATUR.

YES. THE CARDS HAVE TOLD ME ALL ABOUT YOUR PLAN.

LUCIFER.

I CAN'T. I CAN'T LET YOU CONSULT THEM.

I DON'T KNOW WHAT THE DECK'S CAPABLE OF. I DON'T TRUST IT ANYMORE.

LOOK AROUND YOU, MELEOS. YOUR WHOLE LIFE IS FLAMMABLE.

SAYING NO TO ME IS AN OPTION YOU JUST DON'T HAVE.

YES. I... I SEE.

BUT I CAN'T JUST FETCH IT. IT NEEDS TO BE WOKEN. PREPARED.

YOU HAVE UNTIL TONIGHT. I'LL COME AT SUNSET. UNDERSTAND ME, MELEOS. I WILL HAVE THIS DIVINATION.

IF THE CARDS ARE UNAVAILABLE I'LL JUST HAVE TO USE YOUR ENTRAILS.

YOU SPEAK GERMAN, MAN?

YOU SPEAK DEUTSCHER FUCKING LANGUAGE?

YOU ASK US TO STOP IN GERMAN AND WE'LL LEAVE YOU ALONE.

uhhhh!

YOUR MIND WANDERS WHEN YOU'RE ON LOOKOUT.

KARL THINKS: GUNTER ALWAYS SAYS THE SAME THING WHEN HE'S BEATING SOMEONE UP. THE SAME WORDS EXACTLY, LIKE A SCRIPT.

THEN THE TALKING GIVES WAY TO REPETITIVE IMPACT SOUNDS AND HE THINKS ARBEIT MACHT FREI. BUT NOT FOR THE GASTARBEITEN, WHO STEAL OUR JOBS.

MIND YOUR FOOT, ERICH, FOR CHRIST'S SAKE!

WORK IS FOR GERMANS. FREEDOM IS FOR THOSE WHO DESERVE IT.

IT'S HALTEN. HALTEN SIE BITTE. YOU THINK YOU'LL REMEMBER THAT NEXT TIME?

LET'S PISS ON HIM.

DON'T BE STUPID, MAN. HE'S GOING TO DIE. WE SHOULD GET OUT OF HERE.

RAUS

FUCK, NO NEED TO *RUN*, KARL. IT LOOKS BLOODY *SUSPICIOUS*. WE'RE JUST WALKING, OKAY?

YEAH, WHAT ARE *YOU* PANICKING FOR? IT'S NOT LIKE YOU EVEN *DID* ANYTHING.

WHAT DO YOU MEAN? I WENT *LOOKOUT*.

YES, KARL. YOU WENT LOOKOUT. *AGAIN*. WITHOUT BEING *ASKED* TO.

I THOUGHT YOU WANTED TO BE FULLY *INVOLVED* IN THE POLITICAL DIALECTIC.

OF COURSE I DO.

WELL IT'S *EASY*, MAN. YOU JUST BEAT THE *SHIT* OUT OF SOMEBODY WE DON'T LIKE.

IS THAT *OKAY* FOR YOU?

YEAH. IT'S FINE. REALLY.

SO WHO *DON'T* WE LIKE, KARL?

WELL, YOU KNOW...

YEAH, I DO. TELL ME.

JEWS. TURKS. PAKIS. LEFTIES.

QUEERS.

YEAH, YOU GOT TO LOOK OUT FOR THOSE QUEERS, KARL. A GOOD-LOOKING BOY LIKE YOU. BUY YOUR-SELF A CAN OF PAINT AND DO SOME HOMEWORK, OKAY?

YOU'RE IN OR YOU'RE *OUT*. WE DON'T *NEED* A FAN CLUB.

"WE DON'T NEED A FAN CLUB..."

NO, THEY NEED A *SACRIFICE*. AN OFFERING. THE PRICE OF ADMISSION.

AND HE WANTS TO PAY IT. WANTS TO *PROVE* THAT HE BELONGS. THEN HE CAN STEP THROUGH THE DOOR...

...THE ONE MARKED ADULTS ONLY.

NEEDLE'S EYE
PRIVAT KABERATT
BAR

HELLO, JILL. HUGO WAS LOOKING FOR YOU. HE WAS SEEMING PRETTY PISSED OUT.

THAT'S PISSED OFF LOTTE. NEVER MIND HUGO. WHAT ABOUT MR. METTERLINCK? IS HE IN YET?

I DON'T THINK SO. WHY?

I ASKED HIM ABOUT A SOLO SPOT. YOU KNOW, SINGING.

I THINK HE'S GONNA GO FOR IT. THEN HUGO CAN KISS MY RING.

HOW WOULD IT BE IF HUGO JUST WRINGS YOUR NECK?

UMM...YEAH, MAYBE. BUT MY IDEA HAS MORE IMMEDIATE VISUAL APPEAL.

I ASK YOU TO COME AN HOUR EARLY, PETERSON, FOR PRACTICE. BECAUSE EVERY MISTAKE YOU DO LOOKS BAD FOR ME.

I DON'T WANT TO BE WORKING BLOODY HAMBURGER CABARET UNTIL I RETIRE, YOU KNOW?

IT'S PRESTO. JILL PRESTO. I DON'T GO BY PETERSON ANYMORE, HUGO.

YOU CAN CALL YOURSELF THE VIRGIN BLOODY MARY IF YOU WANT TO. BUT YOU MAKE ME LOOK BAD, I FUCKING PAY YOU OFF. YOU UNDERSTAND ME?

RIGHT. WHERE DO WE START?

DOVE IN A FRYING PAN. THEN FLYING KNIVES.

AND SWING FROM THE HIP, AND BEND AT THE KNEE, AND OFF WITH THE LID.

AND ONE TWO THREE FLY. SATISFIED?

NO. SMOOTHER. ONE SMOOTH MOVEMENT. CHRIST.

HEY, HUGO. WHEN I DO MY SOLO ACT... YOU THINK I'D LOOK COOL IN, LIKE, A MASK OVER JUST ONE HALF OF MY FACE?

SOMETHING IS AMISS.

HE THINKS FLEETINGLY OF HIS WINGS. NOSTALGIA OR PREMONITION?

NEW VARIABLES ARE BEING ADDED TO A SITUATION ALREADY COMPLICATED.

HE HAS TO ACT BEFORE ACTION BECOMES IMPOSSIBLE.

...BUT IN THE ABSENCE OF ANYTHING BETTER YOU'LL HAVE TO DO.

THIS IS UNDIGNIFIED...

THERE IS A *DOOR* AT THE BACK OF MELEOS'S SHOP THAT REQUIRES MORE THAN A KEY TO OPEN IT. MOST OF THE TIME IT ISN'T EVEN *VISIBLE*.

PRIVAT

HE NEVER *STANDS* HERE WITHOUT FEELING THE *WEIGHT OF AGES* PRESSING AGAINST THE DOOR FROM THE OTHER SIDE.

THERE IS A CELLAR ROOM IN THE PLANS, IF ANYONE EVER WANTED TO *LOOK*. TWELVE FEET BY FIFTEEN, WITH A SMALL UTILITIES CUPBOARD.

HE COULD *FLY* DOWN, OF COURSE. THE STAIRWELL IS WIDE ENOUGH FOR HIS WINGS, IF HE CHOSE TO MANIFEST THEM.

BUT THE TRUTH IS, HE'S IN NO *HURRY* TO REACH THE BOTTOM.

THERE IS NO *DUST*. HE IS THE *ONLY ONE* WHO EVER COMES HERE AND HE DOES NOT SHED SKIN CELLS SO THERE IS NOTHING OUT OF WHICH DUST COULD BE *MADE*.

HE IS NEAR THE *BOTTOM* NOW. HE IS APPROACHING THE FINAL CHAMBER.

THERE ARE NO BOOKS AT ALL HERE.

AND THE VOICES THAT RISE FROM THIS PLACE ARE NOT EVEN *REMOTELY* HUMAN.

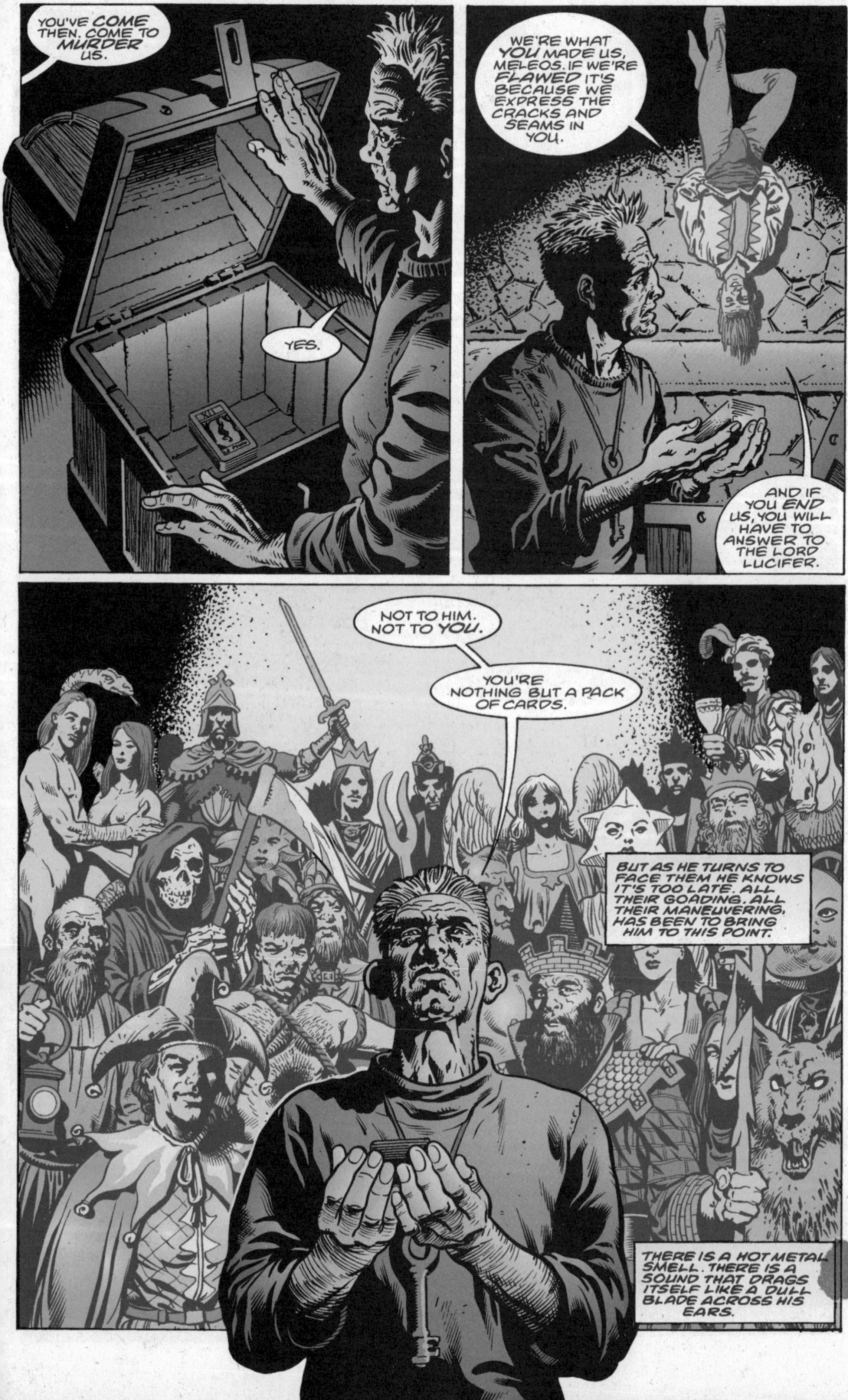
YOU'VE COME THEN. COME TO MURDER US.
YES.
WE'RE WHAT YOU MADE US, MELEOS. IF WE'RE FLAWED IT'S BECAUSE WE EXPRESS THE CRACKS AND SEAMS IN YOU.
AND IF YOU END US, YOU WILL HAVE TO ANSWER TO THE LORD LUCIFER.
NOT TO HIM. NOT TO YOU.
YOU'RE NOTHING BUT A PACK OF CARDS.
BUT AS HE TURNS TO FACE THEM HE KNOWS IT'S TOO LATE. ALL THEIR GOADING. ALL THEIR MANEUVERING, HAS BEEN TO BRING HIM TO THIS POINT.
THERE IS A HOT METAL SMELL. THERE IS A SOUND THAT DRAGS ITSELF LIKE A DULL BLADE ACROSS HIS EARS.

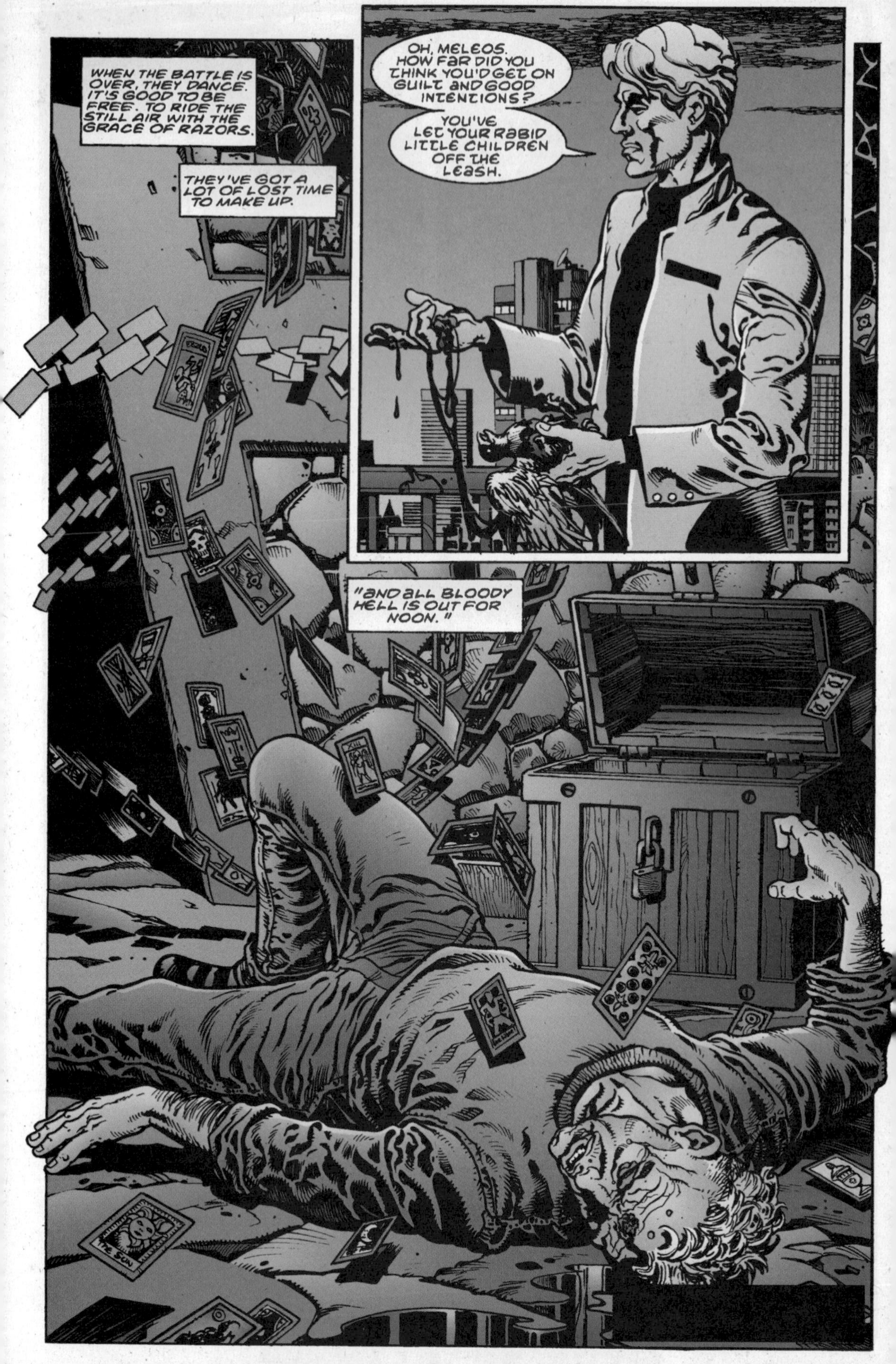
WHEN THE BATTLE IS OVER, THEY DANCE. IT'S GOOD TO BE FREE. TO RIDE THE STILL AIR WITH THE GRACE OF RAZORS.
THEY'VE GOT A LOT OF LOST TIME TO MAKE UP.
OH, MELEOS. HOW FAR DID YOU THINK YOU'D GET ON GUILT AND GOOD INTENTIONS?
YOU'VE LET YOUR RABID LITTLE CHILDREN OFF THE LEASH.
"AND ALL BLOODY HELL IS OUT FOR NOON."

HAMBURG. THE DAWN OF A NEW MILLENNIUM.

A SIX CARD SPREAD

THE SUN

THE LOVERS

RAGE

THE TOWER

TEMPERANCE

DEATH

THE HANGED MAN

THE EMPEROR

THE WHEEL

MIKE CAREY · WRITER   CHRIS WESTON · PENCILLER
JAMES HODGKINS · INKER   DANIEL VOZZO · COLOR & SEPS
ELLIE DE VILLE · LETTERER   DUNCAN FEGREDO · COVER ART
WILL DENNIS · ASST. EDITOR   SHELLY ROEBERG · EDITOR

BASED ON THE CHARACTER CREATED BY
GAIMAN, KIETH & DRINGENBERG

"ARE THEY NOT WONDERFUL, THESE HUMANS, WITH THEIR MAYFLY LIVES AND MAD DREAMS?"

"I WILL CHRONICLE THEM. I WILL BE THE KEEPER OF THEIR MEMORY."

MELEOS'S OWN WORDS. BUT NOW HE IS CRIPPLED FROM HIS FIGHT AGAINST THE CARDS, AND THE CHRONICLE HE HAS MADE IS AN UNDERGROUND TOWER MORE THAN A MILE HIGH.

THE SCAR ON HIS FACE BURNS LIKE A BRAND.

AND IT WILL NOT CLOSE, EVEN THOUGH HE HAS FOCUSED THE FULL FORCE OF HIS WILL UPON IT.

IT IS THE MARK OF HIS SIN.

THE MIND AND THE SOUL TRACE THE *LINE* THAT THE HAND WILL FOLLOW. BUT THE MOVEMENTS THAT THE HAND DOES *NOT* MAKE MATTER JUST AS MUCH.

THE DRAWING MUST SUBSUME ALL *UNDRAWN* LINES AND ALL *POTENTIAL* FIGURES INTO A PERFECT STASIS.

WE'RE FIGHTING FOR FREEDOM, MELEOS. FREEDOM TO DEFINE OUR-SELVES. FREEDOM FROM THE TYRANNY OF PREDESTINATION.

AS AN ARTIST, ISN'T THAT *YOUR* FIGHT TOO?

I DO NOT FIGHT. BUT IT MAY BE THAT I CAN HELP YOU IN *ANOTHER* WAY, LUCIFER.

I VISITED DESTINY OF THE *ANEUTELOI* RECENTLY.

HE WAS NOT... CORDIAL. BUT HE ALLOWED ME TO EXAMINE HIS BOOK.

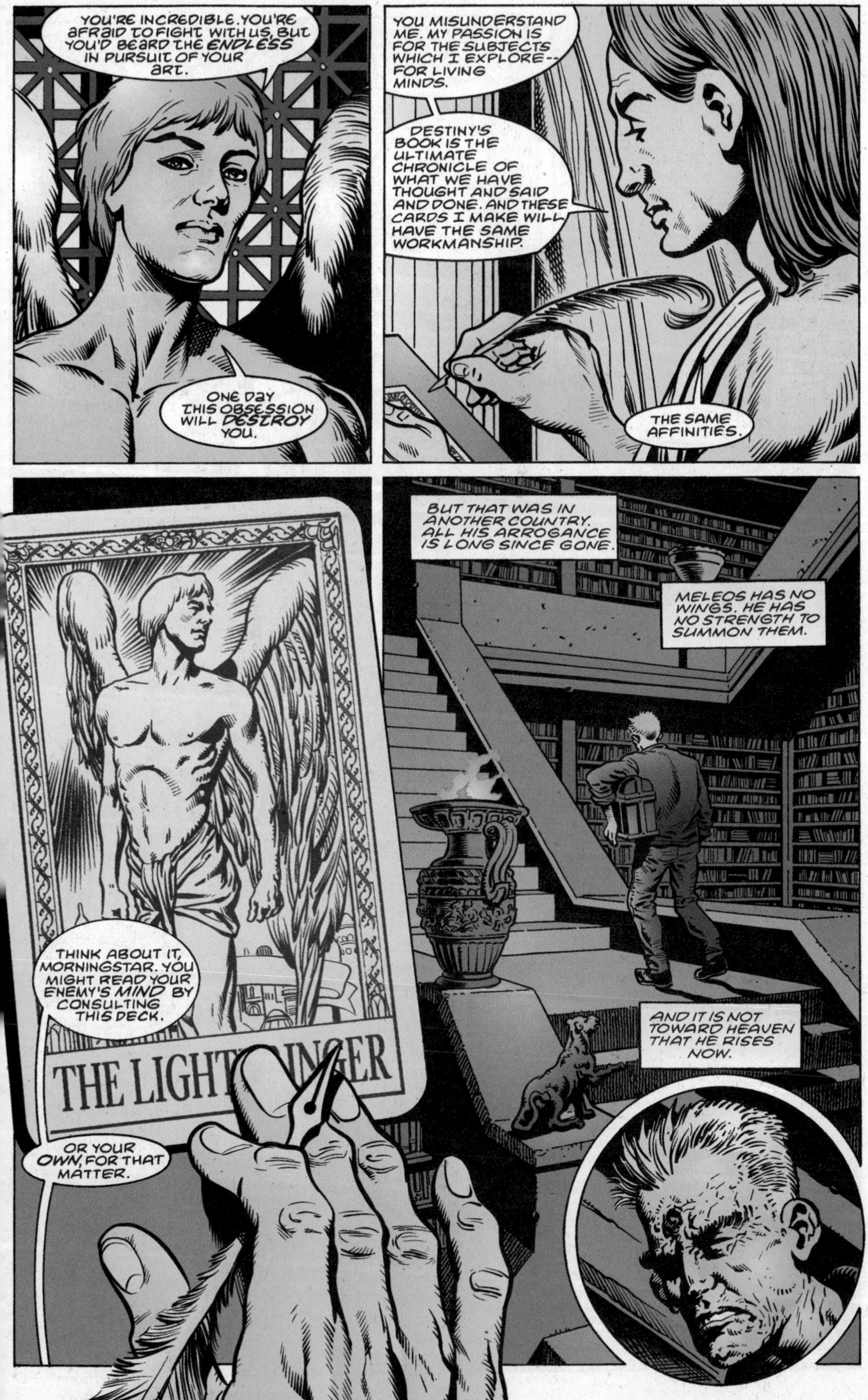

YOU'RE INCREDIBLE. YOU'RE AFRAID TO FIGHT WITH US, BUT YOU'D BEARD THE ENDLESS IN PURSUIT OF YOUR ART.
ONE DAY THIS OBSESSION WILL DESTROY YOU.
YOU MISUNDERSTAND ME. MY PASSION IS FOR THE SUBJECTS WHICH I EXPLORE-- FOR LIVING MINDS.
DESTINY'S BOOK IS THE ULTIMATE CHRONICLE OF WHAT WE HAVE THOUGHT AND SAID AND DONE. AND THESE CARDS I MAKE WILL HAVE THE SAME WORKMANSHIP.
THE SAME AFFINITIES.
THINK ABOUT IT, MORNINGSTAR. YOU MIGHT READ YOUR ENEMY'S MIND BY CONSULTING THIS DECK.
OR YOUR OWN, FOR THAT MATTER.
BUT THAT WAS IN ANOTHER COUNTRY. ALL HIS ARROGANCE IS LONG SINCE GONE.
MELEOS HAS NO WINGS. HE HAS NO STRENGTH TO SUMMON THEM.
AND IT IS NOT TOWARD HEAVEN THAT HE RISES NOW.

CAN YOU GET...UH... WORDS WITH THAT?

YEAH, SURE. THE STANDARD DESIGN HAS *FC ST. PAULI FOREVER*, BUT YOU CAN HAVE WHATEVER YOU LIKE.

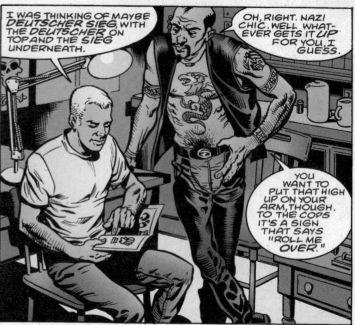

I WAS THINKING OF MAYBE *DEUTSCHER SIEG*, WITH THE *DEUTSCHER* ON TOP AND THE *SIEG* UNDERNEATH.

OH, RIGHT. NAZI CHIC. WELL, WHAT-EVER GETS IT *UP* FOR YOU, I GUESS.

YOU WANT TO PUT THAT HIGH UP ON YOUR ARM, THOUGH. TO THE COPS IT'S A SIGN THAT SAYS "ROLL ME *OVER*."

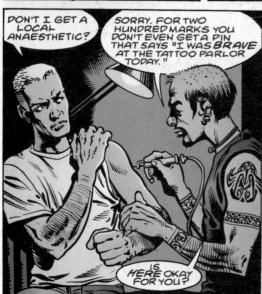

DON'T I GET A LOCAL ANAESTHETIC?

SORRY. FOR TWO HUNDRED MARKS YOU DON'T EVEN GET A PIN THAT SAYS "I WAS *BRAVE* AT THE TATTOO PARLOR TODAY."

IS *HERE* OKAY FOR YOU?

AAH!

AAH!

SCHEISSE!

SWEAR BOX. YOU'D BETTER SAVE THE *CHOICEST* ONES FOR LATER. IT GETS *WORSE* WHEN THE NERVES WAKE UP PROPERLY.

OKAY, MAN! ENOUGH! ENOUGH!

SORRY ABOUT THAT. YOU MUST HAVE A LOW *PAIN* THRESHOLD.

I'LL FINISH IT ANOTHER TIME, OKAY?

THERE'S ALWAYS MARKER, I SUPPOSE.

SHIT, THAT'S NOT EVEN...

WHAT THE FUCK DOES THAT LOOK LIKE, MAN?

SHIT SHIT SHIT SHIT.

NOW, THAT-- THAT'S A REAL TATTOO.

THE EMPEROR

BUT FOR SOMETHING THAT BIG, YOU'D BE LOOKING AT TWO THOUSAND MARKS.

AND YOU'D BE LUCKY IF YOUR WHOLE FUCKING ARM DIDN'T DROP OFF.

BUT WHY WEAR IT WHEN YOU CAN BE IT?

YOU'VE GOT THE SEEDS OF GREATNESS. GUNTER KNOWS. THAT'S WHY HE'S SO HARD ON YOU. HE'S TESTING YOU.

THAT'S WHAT THIS IS ALL ABOUT, SON.

YOU'VE GOT TO PAY THE PRICE OF ADMISSION. YOU SAID SO YOURSELF.

BE DECISIVE. BE STERN AND SWIFT.

"BE MAGNIFICENT."

THE EMPEROR

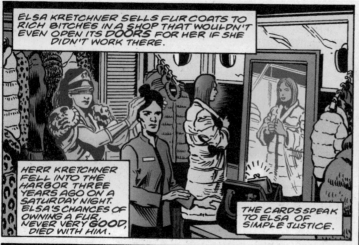

ELSA KRETCHNER SELLS FUR COATS TO RICH BITCHES IN A SHOP THAT WOULDN'T EVEN OPEN ITS DOORS FOR HER IF SHE DIDN'T WORK THERE.

HERR KRETCHNER FELL INTO THE HARBOR THREE YEARS AGO ON A SATURDAY NIGHT. ELSA'S CHANCES OF OWNING A FUR, NEVER VERY GOOD, DIED WITH HIM.

THE CARDS SPEAK TO ELSA OF SIMPLE JUSTICE.

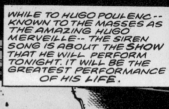

WHILE TO HUGO POULENC-- KNOWN TO THE MASSES AS THE AMAZING HUGO MERVEILLE-- THE SIREN SONG IS ABOUT THE SHOW THAT HE WILL PERFORM TONIGHT. IT WILL BE THE GREATEST PERFORMANCE OF HIS LIFE.

AND OTTO LINDAUER ONCE AGAIN CONFRONTS HIS WIFE, PAULA, WITH THE SEXUAL ACTS HE THINKS SHE HAS PERFORMED WITH HIS WORK COLLEAGUES, THE GARDENER, AND THE CLEANING CREW.

THE UNHEARD VOICES TELL HIM HE HAS A RIGHT TO HIS RAGE.

HE'S READY. HIS CRAFT IS PERFECT. HE WILL JOIN THE CANON AND SIT WITH HARRY AND DAVID IN GLORY FOREVER.

NIEDERHAFEN. ST. PAULI. AUSSENALSTER. THE CHORUS EBBS AND FLOWS WITH THE WIND ALONG THE URBAN CANYONS AND THE ARTERIAL ROADS.

PROMISING. MOCKING. URGING.

PLAYING THE GAME OF THE BASANOS WITH HUMANKIND.

BUT IN THE PARK CALLED THE PLANTEN UN BLOMEN LUCIFER WALKS, WATCHING THE PLAY OF LIGHT ON WATER, THINKING ABOUT FLUX AND PERMANENCE.

AND AROUND HIM, AT LEAST, THERE IS A SANCTIFIED SILENCE.

MAZIKEEN. I'M SORRY TO INTERRUPT SUCH A *SPECIAL* MOMENT, BUT I NEED YOU.

YEHKHHH, RROAHD.

THERE ARE PLACES IN ANY TOWN WHERE SHARPENING A *KNIFE* WILL PASS WITHOUT COMMENT.

GENERALLY SPEAKING, PUBLIC PARKS ARE A *POOR* BET EXCEPT MAYBE IN NEW YORK CITY.

I HHELT I NUKHT VHE *REAGHY*, RROAHD. IHHH RE NUKHT *HHIGHT* HHHE CARGHHS...

WE NEED TO *FIND* THEM BEFORE WE CAN FIGHT THEM. AND WE NEED TO APPROACH THEM ON THEIR *BLIND* SIDE, OR THEY'LL GET SKITTISH AND RUN.

I NEED YOU TO *BLEED* ON THESE LEAVES, AS I HAVE DONE.

I WATCHED MELEOS *DESIGN* THEM. THE *BASANOS* IS AN EXQUISITE PIECE OF WORK, BUT *NO* MAKING IS PERFECT.

IF WE CAST OUR BLOOD ON THE WINDS THEY'LL SEE SHADOWS OF US EVERY-WHERE.

THE VERY *SHARPNESS* OF THEIR SIGHT IS A WEAKNESS WE CAN EXPLOIT.

THERE. NOW I HAVE ONE SMALL MATTER TO ATTEND TO BEFORE WE CAN BEGIN.

NEREOKHH?

MELEOS. OF COURSE.

WE HAVE PERHAPS TWO HOURS. I'LL GIVE HIM THE FIRST TEN MINUTES.

AND THEN WE'LL *HUNT*.

AUSGANG

THE NEEDLE'S EYE.

ANY SIGN OF MR. METTERLINCK, LOTTE?

HE CAME *IN*, JILL. I DON'T KNOW WHERE HE IS *NOW*, THOUGH. DID YOU TRY THE BAR?

YEAH. TWICE.

HER INTERIOR SOUNDTRACK IS THE SAME AS IT'S EVER BEEN FOR ALL THE YEARS OF SLAMMED DOORS AND SCUT WORK.

IF IT'S A LITTLE FAINTER NOW, THAT'S ONLY BECAUSE SHE'S TIRED.

HEY, HUGO, DID YOU SEE METZ YET TONIGHT?

DID I....?DID I *WHAT*?

NO, PETERSON, I DIDN'T SEE HIM. WHAT ARE YOU WANTING TO DO, ANYWAY, TO COME IN WITHOUT KNOCKING?

GIVE ME SOME FUCKING *PRIVACY*, WOULD YOU MIND? AND CLOSE THE DOOR!

FUCK YOUR MOTHER, HUGO.

IF YOU DIDN'T *ALREADY*.

SLAM

JILL WILL BE HIS HANDMAIDEN, THE VOICES WHISPER.

AND, AT LONG LAST SHE'LL LEARN TO SHOW THE PROPER RESPECT.

HA! CAUGHT YOU.

OOPS. SORRY, SOLA.

UH... THAT'S OKAY, JILL.

I'LL SEE YOU LATER, MAYBE. I HAVE TO PRACTICE MY NUMBER.

GIVEN THAT SHE'S A STRIPPER SHE WAS GETTING PLENTY OF PRACTICE RIGHT HERE, WASN'T SHE?

IS THIS SOMETHING THAT CAN WAIT, JILL? YOU'VE PICKED A LOUSY TIME.

I JUST WANTED TO ASK ABOUT MY SOLO SPOT--

I CAN'T THINK ABOUT IT JUST YET. I'VE GOT A DEPOSITION TO MAKE TO PETRA'S LAWYER TOMORROW.

AND NOW SHE SAYS SHE'S GOING TO SUE FOR CUSTODY OF MAX.

OH. YEAH. LOTTE TOLD ME THAT.

I'M SORRY, METZ, THAT'S REALLY...

HOLD ON THERE, BALD EAGLE. LOTTE TOLD ME PETRA SERVED YOU THOSE PAPERS THREE WEEKS AGO. SO WHY ARE YOU BRINGING THEM UP NOW?

WELL IT'S ON MY MIND A LOT. I KEEP--

BULLSHIT.

YOU USED YOUR *PRIVATE* LIFE TO CHANGE THE SUBJECT ON ME, METZ. FOR ABOUT THE *FIFTH* TIME.

NOW GIVE ME A *STRAIGHT* ANSWER.

OKAY, JILL. THE *STRAIGHT* ANSWER.

YOU'RE NOT *UP* TO IT. YOU *SING* OKAY, BUT YOUR *MOVES* ARE AWKWARD AND YOU DON'T PROJECT YOUR *PERSONALITY* ALL THAT WELL.

MY MOVES? *SONOFABITCH!* WHAT ABOUT *YOUR* MOVES? YOU ONLY GAVE SOLA HER BIG CAGE ROUTINE BECAUSE SHE WENT DOWN ON YOU!

ON SECOND THOUGHT, YOU PROJECT JUST *FINE*-- YOU COME ACROSS AS *LOUD* AND *COARSE*.

COARSE? YOU WANNA SEE *COARSE?*

GIMME MY *COAT*, LOTTE. I NEED A DRINK.

JUST WAIT UNTIL I FINISH THIS *PARA-GRAPH*--

HIS WIFE DIES OF LEUKEMIA AND HE MARRIES THE NURSE, OKAY?

YOU'RE ON AT TEN THIRTY, YOU KNOW. I COULD GET YOU A DRINK FROM THE BAR.

THEN THE NURSE *DIVORCES* HIM AND HE SPENDS THE REST OF HIS BEER-BELLIED LIFE FUCKING EIGHTEEN-YEAR-OLD STRIPPERS.

IT'S BASED ON A TRUE STORY. RIGHT METZ?

LOTTE--

--GO INTO THE OFFICE AND TYPE UP A *TERMINATION* LETTER.

"AND LEAVE SOME SPACES FOR ADJECTIVES."

OKAY, DAD, I'M BACK.

JAYESH, THANK GOD YOU'RE HERE. THERE IS A SKIN-HEAD IN THE MIDDLE AISLE. A SKIN-HEAD!

I ASKED IF I COULD HELP HIM AND HE GAVE ME FOUL LANGUAGE! CALL THE POLICE, YAAH.

SHIT! THE POLICE WON'T DO ANYTHING. THEY NEVER DO.

LEAVE HIM TO ME.

LISTEN, MY FRIEND, MY DAD'S ALREADY CALLED THE POLICE, SO IF YOU DON'T MIND...

FUCK.

KARL...

DEVA. DO YOU HAVE ANY ANTISEPTIC OINTMENT? I... I CUT MY ARM AND IT'S SWOLLEN UP.

SURE. SURE WE DO.

YEAH, HERE WE GO. ELOTOX -- DISINFECTS MINOR WOUNDS AND RELIEVES ITCHING. DO YOU HAVE AN ITCH?

NO. I TOLD YOU. A SWELLING, NOT AN ITCH.

AND OH FUCK, JAYESH THINKS, THE HAIRS IN HIS EAR, THE SLIDING OF THAT MUSCLE IN HIS ARM.

THANKS.

AND HE THINKS HE'LL NEVER...

KARL...

...IF HE DOESN'T DO IT NOW.

I WAS WONDERING...UMM...IF YOU...

WHAT?

WELL, YOU KNOW...

...IF YOU'D LIKE TO COME OUT FOR A *DRINK* LATER.

HAH. THAT'S FUNNY, YOU KNOW? AFTER A DAY LIKE THIS.

YEAH, SURE A DRINK. WHY NOT?

REALLY?

YES, REALLY. THEN MAYBE YOU'LL GIVE ME SOME FUCKING *PEACE.*

LISTEN, JAYESH. I'VE GOT FRIENDS THAT'LL LITERALLY FUCKING *KILL* ME IF THEY SEE US TOGETHER.

MEET ME AT THE *BACK* DOOR OF THE SHOP AT TEN. NOT ON THE STREET.

RIGHT. OKAY.

TCHAH. HE IS A ROUGH ELEMENT. AND A RACIST. HE HAS A FOUL TONGUE.

YEAH...

...AND HAIRY EARS.

"I WILL CHRONICLE THEM," HE HAD SAID.

NOW ONE OF THE TOOLS HE MADE HAS SPILLED RED INK ACROSS THE PAGES OF THE CHRONICLE, AND HE IS LEFT STARING HELPLESSLY AT HIS STAINED HANDS.

I'M SORRY. I'M SO SORRY...

...PLEASE...

GOOD EVENING, MELEOS. I WAS BEGINNING TO WONDER IF YOU'D *MAKE* IT. THOSE LAST TWENTY FLIGHTS NEARLY *FINISHED* YOU.

TWO COPIES OF JEROME'S BIBLE MIGHT BE SEEN AS EXCESSIVE, EVEN IF ONE *DOES* HAVE A PSALM MISSING.

DID THE *BASANOS* DO THAT TO YOUR FACE?

WE FOUGHT. THEY... THEY *BROKE* MY CONCENTRATION, AND THEN STRUCK ME *DOWN*. AND NOW I CAN'T HEAL THE WOUND.

LUCIFER, THEY'RE *FREE*. THEY'VE *ESCAPED* FROM ME.

I KNOW. THAT'S WHY I'M HERE.

YOU THOUGHT YOU COULD TRAP THEM AGAIN IN THE *SAME* BOX.

DON'T YOU KNOW THE PROVERB ABOUT *WORMS* AND *CANS?*

KRRAAK

WHAT SHOULD I DO WITH YOU, MELEOS? I NEED SOMETHING QUICK BUT UNFORGETTABLE.

I WASN'T *TRYING* TO SET THEM FREE! I WANTED TO *KILL* THEM! YOU MUST *KNOW* THAT!

YOU *DISOBEYED* ME. THAT'S THE ISSUE AS I SEE IT.

I WOULD HAVE DONE A SIMPLE SIX-CARD SPREAD, AND THEN I WOULD HAVE *GONE*.

IT WOULD HAVE BEEN *PAINLESS*, COMPARATIVELY.

AND WHAT IF THEY'D OVER-POWERED YOU? THEY MIGHT HAVE--

ESCAPED? YOU'RE A FOOL, MELEOS.

I'VE SAVED EVERY *WORD* THAT HUMANKIND HAS WRITTEN, WHETHER ON STONE OR SLATE OR PAPER. AND NOT CONTENT WITH THAT, I THOUGHT TO RECORD THEIR *THOUGHTS* AS WELL.

THAT'S WHY I BROUGHT THE CARDS HERE. THAT'S WHY I LET THEM CATCH THE *SCENT* OF HUMANITY.

I'M *WORSE* THAN A FOOL.

I SUPPOSE IT'S BECAUSE WE DON'T *BREED* THAT WE PUT SO MUCH OF OURSELVES INTO OUR *TOOLS*.

FROM ONE POINT OF VIEW YOU'VE ALREADY PUNISHED YOURSELF ENOUGH.

SO DON'T SEE THIS AS A PUNISH-MENT.

SEE IT AS AN HONEST CRITIQUE OF YOUR... PROJECT.

WHAT HAVE YOU *DONE*, LUCIFER, PLEASE! TELL ME!

YOU HAVE A FINE MIND, MELEOS.

PROCEED BY *OBSERVATION* AND *INFERENCE*.

AND THE CHILD WALKS AMONG THE YOUNG, TIRED WHORES ON THE REEPERBAHN,' LOOKING INTO EVERY FACE. SHE IS SEARCHING, AND SO SHE IS FULLY INCARNATE.

SHE IS SEARCHING, AND SO SHE HAS NO TIME TO PLAY. BUT TO PLAY IS TO FEEL YOURSELF ALIVE; TO WEAVE THE INVISIBLE THREADS OF FATE INTO FANTASTIC PATTERNS THAT NO ONE ELSE CAN SEE.

FOR HER KIND IT IS SEX AND FOOD AND REST--THE ONLY IMPERATIVE.

HER CARD IS INNOCENCE. BUT THAT IS NOT A SIGN THAT DEFINES HER. IT IS A DRESS SHE WEARS.

WHERE SHE WALKS, THE STREET GIRLS ARE ASSAILED BY MEMORIES. ALL THE STATIONS OF THE NIGHT. ALL THE MOMENTS OF SURRENDER AND DEGRADATION.

WHILE THE MEN IN THE CARS WITH THE WINDOWS ROLLED DOWN CRASH SICKENINGLY INTO SELF-KNOWLEDGE. EVEN AT FIVE MILES AN HOUR THEY HAVE NO TIME TO SWERVE.

FOR THE EYES OF INNOCENCE SEE ALL THINGS ANEW, AND THE VEILS OF CUSTOM AND SELF-DECEIT ARE TORN AWAY AS THOUGH THEY HAD NEVER BEEN.

SORRY, KID. YOU CAN'T COME THROUGH HERE.

GET ME ANOTHER DRESSING!

SHIT, WHY WOULD A MAN POKE HIS OWN EYES OUT?

HE PUT HIS EYES OUT BECAUSE HE DIDN'T WANT TO SEE.

GET THESE PEOPLE MOVING, GERD. WHAT WAS THAT, LOVE?

IT WILL BE DIFFERENT FOR YOU. YOU'LL WANT TO PASS THE PAIN ON TO SOMEBODY ELSE.

THERE IS A TRILLING IN THE WIRES--A HIGH, INHUMAN SOUND.

A MILLION CATS ARE MEWLING IN A MILLION HYPOTHETICAL BOXES. A MILLION TRIGGERS ARE PULLED.

DESTINY RIDES ON THE BULLETS.

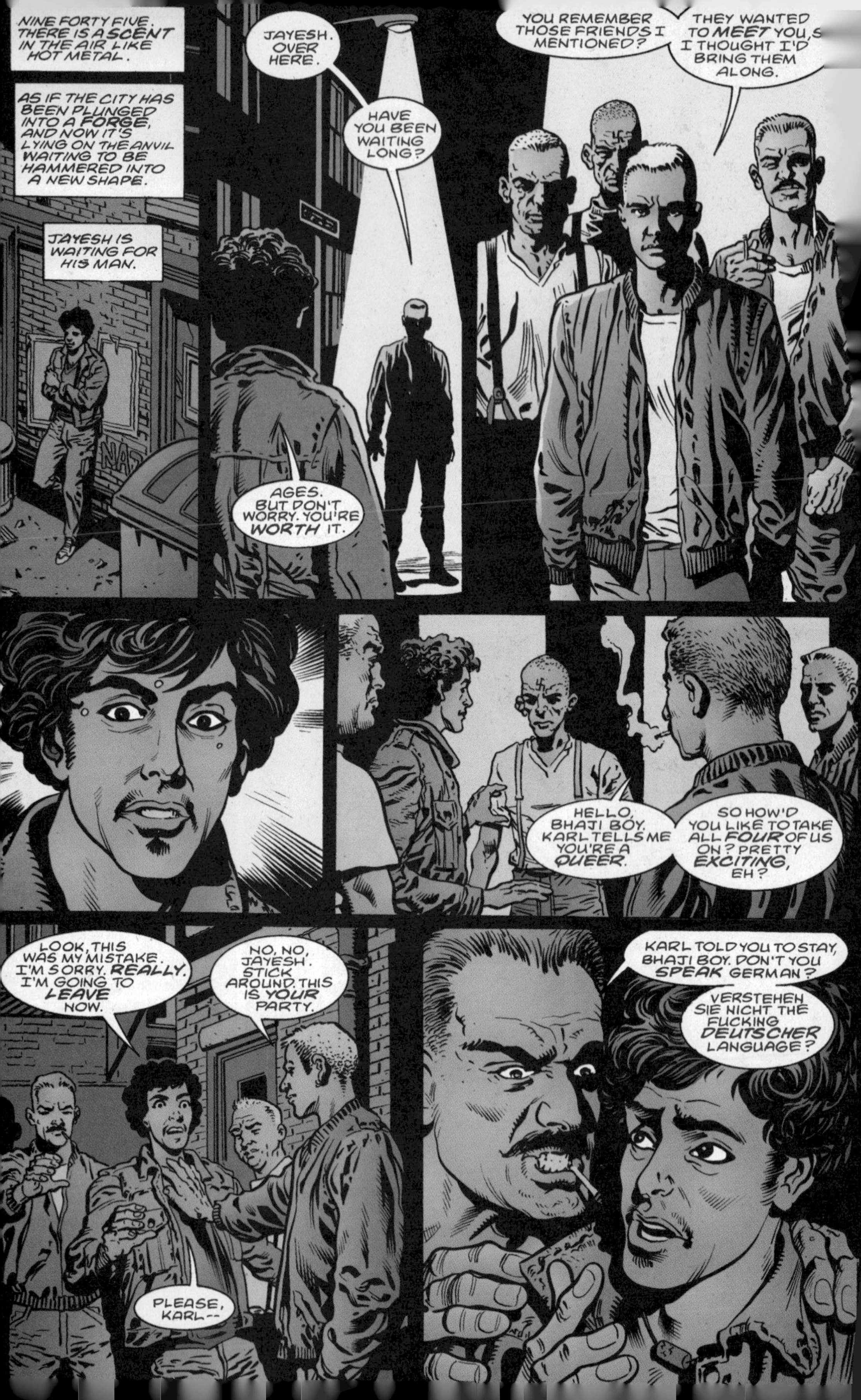
NINE FORTY FIVE. THERE IS A SCENT IN THE AIR LIKE HOT METAL.
AS IF THE CITY HAS BEEN PLUNGED INTO A FORGE, AND NOW IT'S LYING ON THE ANVIL WAITING TO BE HAMMERED INTO A NEW SHAPE.
JAYESH IS WAITING FOR HIS MAN.
JAYESH. OVER HERE.
HAVE YOU BEEN WAITING LONG?
AGES. BUT DON'T WORRY. YOU'RE WORTH IT.
YOU REMEMBER THOSE FRIENDS I MENTIONED?
THEY WANTED TO MEET YOU, SO I THOUGHT I'D BRING THEM ALONG.
HELLO, BHAJI BOY. KARL TELLS ME YOU'RE A QUEER.
SO HOW'D YOU LIKE TO TAKE ALL FOUR OF US ON? PRETTY EXCITING, EH?
LOOK, THIS WAS MY MISTAKE. I'M SORRY. REALLY. I'M GOING TO LEAVE NOW.
NO, NO, JAYESH. STICK AROUND. THIS IS YOUR PARTY.
PLEASE, KARL--
KARL TOLD YOU TO STAY, BHAJI BOY. DON'T YOU SPEAK GERMAN?
VERSTEHEN SIE NICHT THE FUCKING DEUTSCHER LANGUAGE?

THE MUFFLED **SCREAM**. THE SCUFFLING FEET. THE SMACK AND THUD OF HUMAN FLESH BEING TESTED TO DESTRUCTION. THE SOUNDS ARE SOFT BUT UNMISTAKABLE.

NO. OH NO.

BUT MELEOS DOESN'T **HEAR** THEM.

SURELY... IT'S ONLY THE ONE BOOK. THE ONE HE TOUCHED. THIS IS SOME SORT OF WARNING.

PLEASE... PLEASE DON'T...

BUT NO. LUCIFER DOES NOT **THREATEN** BEFORE HE STRIKES.

FROM LEVEL TO LEVEL HE RUNS. SPINOZA, ARISTOTLE, LAO-TZU...

THE FRAGILE LINES LIKE OPENED **ARTERIES** OF THOUGHT RUN OFF THEIR PAGES AND **POOL** ON THE FLOOR.

THEY HAVE BEEN STRUCK DOWN BY A HEMORRHAGIC **PLAGUE**.

LUCIFER'S **PLAGUE**. FOR HE IS **OLDER** THAN THE ANGEL OF DEATH, AND GREATER.

MORNINGSTAR--

AND WHEN HE COMES IN **JUDGMENT** HE SPARES NONE.

TOO CRUEL...EVEN FOR YOU.

MELEOS KNEELS AMONG THE VIOLATED BODIES OF HIS CHILDREN. TO MOURN THEM ALL WILL TAKE A LIFETIME.

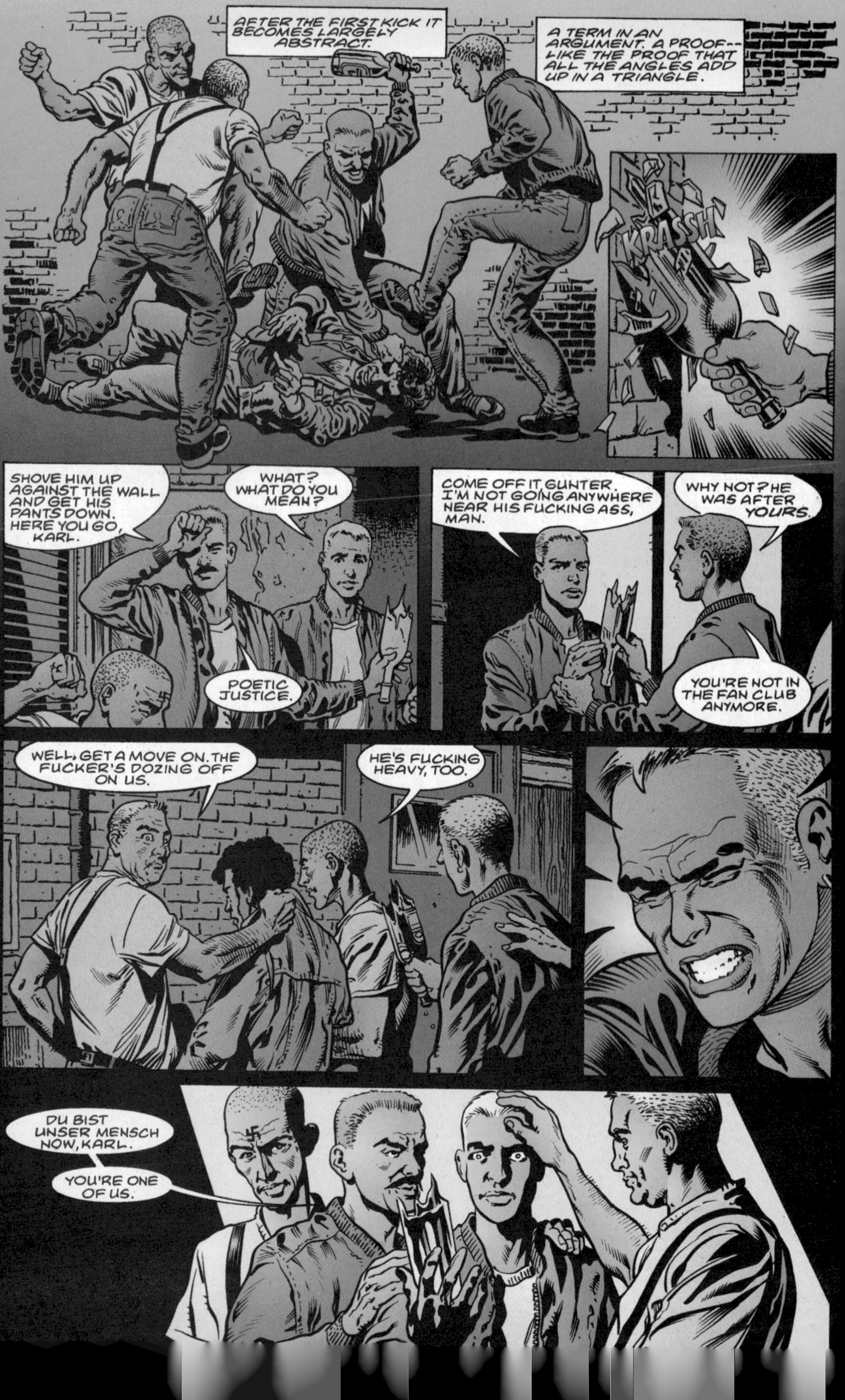
AFTER THE FIRST KICK IT BECOMES LARGELY ABSTRACT.
A TERM IN AN ARGUMENT. A PROOF-- LIKE THE PROOF THAT ALL THE ANGLES ADD UP IN A TRIANGLE.
KRASSH
SHOVE HIM UP AGAINST THE WALL AND GET HIS PANTS DOWN. HERE YOU GO, KARL.
WHAT? WHAT DO YOU MEAN?
POETIC JUSTICE.
COME OFF IT, GUNTER. I'M NOT GOING ANYWHERE NEAR HIS FUCKING ASS, MAN.
WHY NOT? HE WAS AFTER YOURS.
YOU'RE NOT IN THE FAN CLUB ANYMORE.
WELL, GET A MOVE ON. THE FUCKER'S DOZING OFF ON US.
HE'S FUCKING HEAVY, TOO.
DU BIST UNSER MENSCH NOW, KARL.
YOU'RE ONE OF US.

IN MOVIES WHEN YOU'RE *DOWN*, THE BARMAN LISTENS TO ALL YOUR PROBLEMS.

DISPENSES HOMESPUN *WISDOM* WHILE HE'S CLEANING GLASSES WITH A CHECKERED CLOTH.

BUT THIS ISN'T HER COUNTRY, AND THERE ISN'T *ANYONE* WHO KNOWS HER *FUCKING* NAME.

HEY. HEY, GIRL. YOU'VE GOT *STAR* QUALITY, REMEMBER.

YOU DIDN'T COME ALL THE WAY FROM PITTSBURGH JUST TO ROLL OVER AND *BEG* WHEN SOME...

...SOME *SWEAT-STAINED* FLEAPIT WHORE-RUNNER SNAPS HIS FINGERS.

DO YOU WANT ANOTHER *DRINK*, FRAULEIN?

NAH. WHEN YOU START GIVING PEP TALKS TO YOUR *REFLECTION* IT'S PROBABLY TIME TO QUIT.

JUST POINT ME TO THE TOILETS.

SERVE HUGO RIGHT IF HE HAD TO WIGGLE HIS *OWN* ASS AT THE CHEAP SEATS TONIGHT.

BUT I GUESS THE SHOW MUST GO ON.

HELLO. YOU'RE JILL PRESTO, AREN'T YOU? THE *CABARET* STAR?

HUH?

HEY.

AREN'T YOU A LITTLE *YOUNG* TO BE IN HERE?

OH, DON'T WORRY. I'M HERE WITH *FRIENDS*.

WE'RE COMING TO SEE YOUR *ACT* TONIGHT. WE'RE REALLY LOOKING FORWARD TO IT.

WELL THAT'S VERY *FLATTERING*, KIDDO, BUT THE NEEDLE'S EYE IS ADULTS ONLY.

GOD-- I CAN'T BELIEVE YOU KNOW MY *STUFF.*

WE KNOW *EVERYTHING* ABOUT YOU, JILL. YOU SEE, WE'VE SORT OF BEEN AUDITIONING. LOOKING FOR SOMEONE TO *WORK* WITH.

YEAH? WHAT SORT OF ACT?

VARIETY. *LIMITLESS* VARIETY. ALL WE NEED IS A *HOST.* TAKE A LOOK.

YOU MEAN AN M.C.? THAT REALLY DOESN'T SOUND LIKE MY *LINE.*

UMMM... WHAT AM I MEANT TO BE *LOOKING* AT?

YOUR *FUTURE.* YOUR PAST. YOUR *DESTINY.* CAN'T YOU *SEE?*

CUTE, BUT WEIRD. ARE YOU A LITTLE CULT KID? DO YOUR FOLKS SELL *FLOWERS* AT MAJOR AIRPORTS?

LOOK, YOU CAN *KEEP* THE CARDS. I'M NOT INTERESTED.

YOU'VE ALREADY *ACCEPTED* THEM, JILL. DON'T BE AFRAID-- THE DEATH CARD STANDS FOR *CHANGE* AND *REBIRTH.* IT'S A GOOD OMEN.

WHAT *DIES* IS JUST THE PART OF YOU YOU DON'T *NEED* ANYMORE.

I FEEL AS THOUGH I'M *AWAKENING* FROM A LONG SLEEP. TWICE NOW I'VE WALKED *OUT* ON HIM, AND THEN BOTH TIMES I'VE LET HIM *RECAST* ME -- FIND ME A NEW ROLE IN THE UNFOLDING DRAMA.

AND EVERY TIME I TRY TO *IMPROVISE* I FIND MY MOVES WERE RIGHT THERE IN THE *SCRIPT* ALL ALONG.

BUT HIS OMNISCIENCE ONLY *WORKS* BECAUSE THERE ARE NO ALTERNATIVES. I SEE THAT NOW.

AND I HAVE CONCEIVED OF A *REVOLUTION* THAT MAY SURPRISE EVEN HIM.

NGY RROAHD, KHARGHON NE. IFH THIKH NOTHHH THE TINE TO *HHHTRIKE?* RRHILE THHEY ARE DIKHHRACTED?

NO. NOT YET.

KAISER BEE

AUSGANG

WE CAN'T MOVE UNTIL THEY'RE ALL *TOGETHER* IN ONE PLACE. THEY'VE BEEN WINDOW SHOPPING.

AND NOW I THINK THEY'VE DECIDED TO BUY.

WATCH CLOSELY.

THIS IS ONE YOU PROBABLY HAVEN'T SEEN BEFORE.

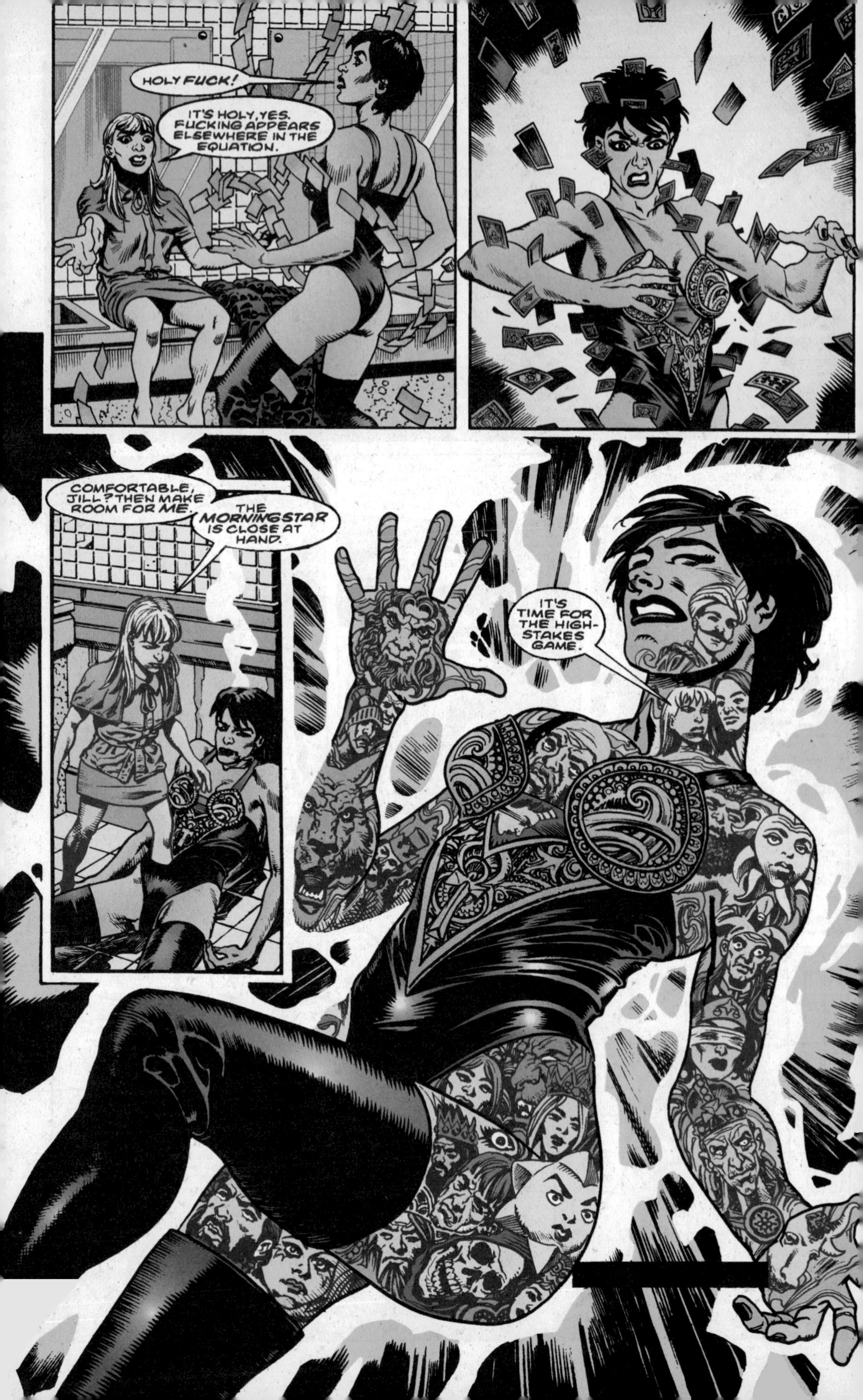
HOLY FUCK!
IT'S HOLY, YES. FUCKING APPEARS ELSEWHERE IN THE EQUATION.
COMFORTABLE, JILL? THEN MAKE ROOM FOR ME.
THE MORNINGSTAR IS CLOSE AT HAND.
IT'S TIME FOR THE HIGH-STAKES GAME.

THE NEEDLE'S EYE. HOW ABOUT THAT. SHE MADE IT.

JILL PRESTO NEVER MISSED A GIG IN HER LIFE, AND SHE'S NOT ABOUT TO START NOW.

STAGE DOOR

WHOA! WHAT'S THIS? WHO SAID *YOU* COULD PINCH-HIT FOR ME?

JILL! YOU CAME BACK. I THOUGHT--

--METZ SAID--

GO FUCK YOURSELF, SOLA. IT'S THE ONLY OPTION YOU HAVEN'T *TRIED.* ISN'T IT?

COME SNIFFING AROUND MY JOB AGAIN, I'LL STRIP YOUR *ASSETS.*

BUT GRAVITY, DAMEN UND HERREN, IS AN *ILLUSION.*

IT IS PART OF *MAYA,* THE GRAND ILLUSION THAT IS THE WORLD.

LET ME SHOW YOU THE TRUTH.

HI. REMEMBER ME?

...

HUGO'S A TROOPER. SKIPS ONE BEAT, THEN ROLLS WITH THE PUNCH AND JUST GETS ON WITH IT.

GIVES HER TIME TO PULL HERSELF TOGETHER. ONLY...

...ONLY HER MIND IS WANDERING.

WELCOME TO Fabulous S...

EILEEN PENN
VEGAS 1979

"Got the world on a string."

STAGE SCHOOL? WHY THE FUCK WOULD YOU WANT TO GO THERE?

I DON'T KNOW. I JUST...

YOU JUST THOUGHT IMITATION WAS THE SINCEREST FORM OF COP-OUT.

CHRIST, YOU'RE YOUR FATHER'S DAUGHTER, AREN'T YOU?

FOLLOW THE DREAM. EVEN IF IT TAKES YOU UP SOMEONE ELSE'S ASS.

LAS VEGAS. 1979.

THE WORLD.

ON A STRING.

A SIX-CARD SPREAD

MIKE CAREY · WRITER   CHRIS WESTON · PENCILLER + INKER PPS. 14,17-19,21   JAMES HODGKINS ·
INKER PPS. 1-13, 15-16, 20,22   DANIEL VOZZO · COLOR + SEPS   ELLIE DE VILLE · LETTERER
DUNCAN FEGREDO · COVER ART   WILL DENNIS · ASST EDITOR   SHELLY ROEBERG · EDITOR
BASED ON THE CHARACTER CREATED BY GAIMAN, KIETH AND DRINGENBERG

I'M AFRAID THE CLUB IS **MEMBERS** ONLY. WOULD YOU LIKE TO JOIN?

I WOULD LIKE YOU TO **REMOVE** YOUR HAND.

OR IF YOU HAVE A CONCESSIONARY TICKET, THEN I COULD--

I DON'T HAVE THE *TIME* FOR THIS.

WHICH FOR YOU IS SOMETHING OF A MIXED BLESSING. EXCUSE ME.

GUUUH!

HUUUULCH!

118

AUSGANG

GUNTER, YOU'VE GOT THE FUCKING *BALLS*, MAN. I CAN'T BELIEVE THEY LET US IN.

YEAH, I GOT THE CARD FROM SOME *OSTDEUTSCHE* SLAG I WAS POKING.

HEY, *KARL*.

YOU WANT ANOTHER *BOTTLE*?

CHRIST, GUNTER. DON'T.

A HANDFUL OF *FEATHERS*, DAMEN UND HERREN. SOME COOKING FAT...

NO MORE THAN THAT. BUT SEE WHAT AN EXOTIC *DISH* WE CAN COOK UP FROM THESE MODEST INGREDIENTS.

ARE YOU MADE OF WOOD?

SORRY, HUGO. I... I FEEL--

GIVE ME SOME *COMMITMENT*, YOU STUPID *BITCH*!

GIVE ME ALL YOU'VE *GOT*!

GO AHEAD, JILL. WHY *NOT*?

YOU CAN'T HOLD IT *IN* MUCH LONGER ANYWAY.

FUCK, MAN, THAT WAS PRETTY *IMPRESSIVE*.

YEAH, IT WAS OKAY. WHERE ARE YOU GOING, KARL?

I NEED TO PISS.

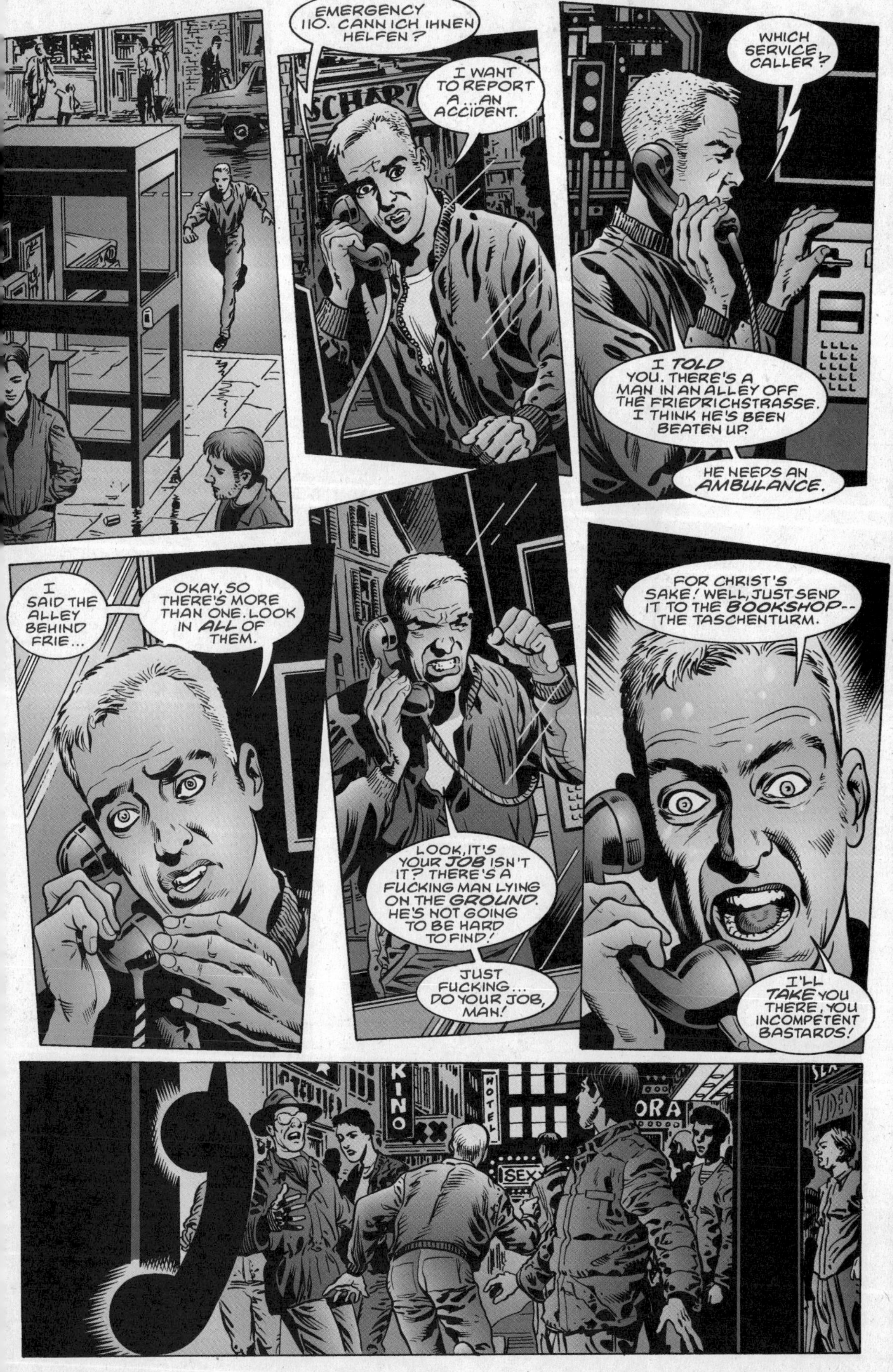
EMERGENCY 110. CANN ICH IHNEN HELFEN?
I WANT TO REPORT A...AN ACCIDENT.
WHICH SERVICE, CALLER?
I TOLD YOU. THERE'S A MAN IN AN ALLEY OFF THE FRIEDRICHSTRASSE. I THINK HE'S BEEN BEATEN UP.
HE NEEDS AN AMBULANCE.
I SAID THE ALLEY BEHIND FRIE...
OKAY, SO THERE'S MORE THAN ONE. LOOK IN ALL OF THEM.
LOOK, IT'S YOUR JOB ISN'T IT? THERE'S A FUCKING MAN LYING ON THE GROUND. HE'S NOT GOING TO BE HARD TO FIND!
JUST FUCKING... DO YOUR JOB, MAN!
FOR CHRIST'S SAKE! WELL, JUST SEND IT TO THE BOOKSHOP-- THE TASCHENTURM.
I'LL TAKE YOU THERE, YOU INCOMPETENT BASTARDS!
KINO
HOTEL
SEX

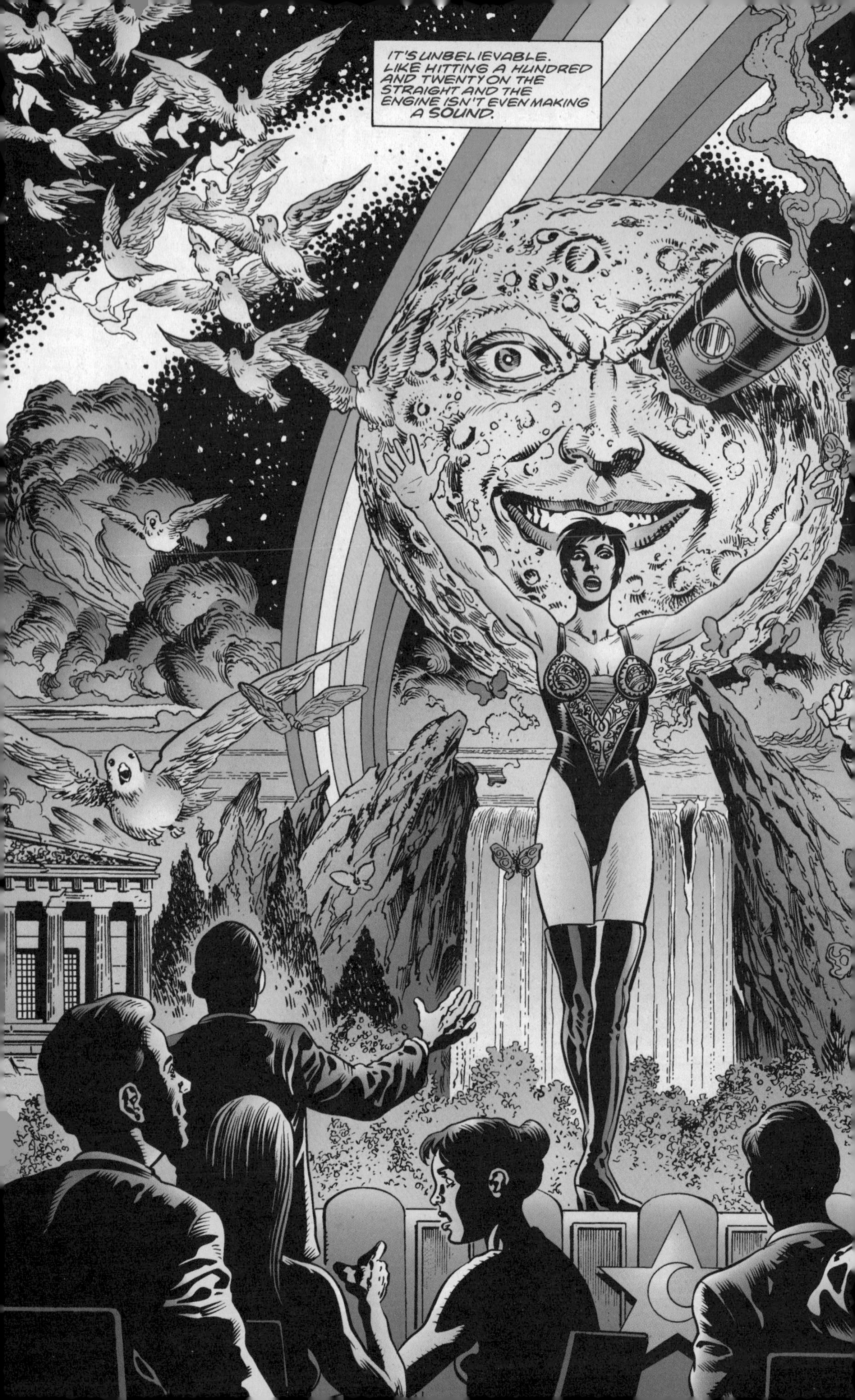
IT'S UNBELIEVABLE. LIKE HITTING A HUNDRED AND TWENTY ON THE STRAIGHT AND THE ENGINE ISN'T EVEN MAKING A SOUND.

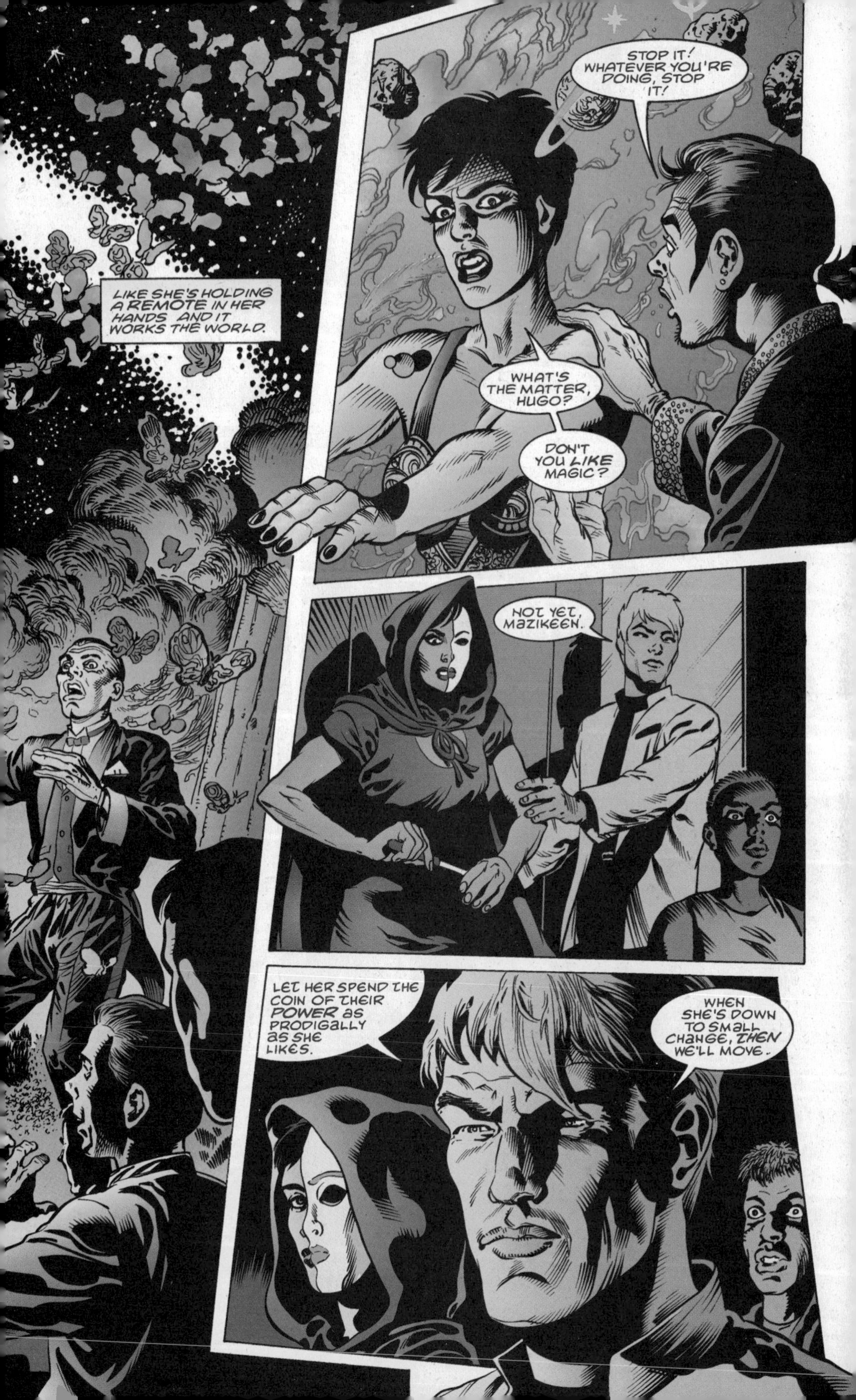
LIKE SHE'S HOLDING A REMOTE IN HER HANDS AND IT WORKS THE WORLD.
STOP IT! WHATEVER YOU'RE DOING, STOP IT!
WHAT'S THE MATTER, HUGO?
DON'T YOU LIKE MAGIC?
NOT YET, MAZIKEEN.
LET HER SPEND THE COIN OF THEIR POWER AS PRODIGALLY AS SHE LIKES.
WHEN SHE'S DOWN TO SMALL CHANGE, THEN WE'LL MOVE.

THIS IS WHAT GOD FELT LIKE WHEN HE MADE THE WORLD.

THIS IS WHY HE DID IT. FOR THE POWER. FOR THE HIGH.

SHE CAN SEE THEIR LIVES. THE PAST STRAIGHT LIKE A WIRE, THE FUTURE BRANCHING INTO A MILLION FILAMENTS.

WHAT THEY ARE AND WERE AND COULD BE.

AND INSIDE THEM... IN THEIR MINDS...

SHE CAN SEE THAT TOO.

HUGO. CHOKING ON TEARS OF ANGER AND HUMILIATION. HE'S THINKING "THE BEST PERFORMANCE OF MY LIFE." AGAIN AND AGAIN.

METZ WANTS TO TEAR UP THE LETTER THAT TELLS HER SHE'S UNEMPLOYED.

HE'S THINKING NUMBERS.

ALL THIS BEAUTY AND STRANGENESS FLATTENED BETWEEN THE COLUMNS OF A BALANCE SHEET.

AND THERE'S LOTTE. WHY ISN'T SHE READING HER CRUDDY ROMANCE? SHE'S THINKING ABOUT A PAIR OF EYES SHE STARED INTO. IT WAS HALF AN HOUR AGO AND SHE STILL CAN'T LOOK AWAY.

SHE'S SEEING THE WORLD THROUGH A HUNDRED STAINED GLASS WINDOWS.

THERE ARE NO BARRIERS. NO DISGUISES. THERE'S NOTHING

NOTHING SHE CAN'T

SEE.

AND SHE BECOMES A LIGHTNING ROD. THE POTENTIAL FUTURES MOVING THROUGH HER INTO THE PRESENT.

SHE FINDS THEIR PAIN. SHE FINDS THEIR DEATHS. THE CURRENT FLOWS.

THE FIRST ONE'S ERICH. THREE YEARS FROM NOW, THERE'S A STRONG POSSIBILITY THAT HE'LL CRASH HIS CAR ON THE AUTOBAHN, DRIVING WITHOUT A SEATBELT.

THE ONE NAMED ECKERHART COULD MEET A RAZOR GANG IN BERLIN WHEN HE'S CELEBRATING THE NEW YEAR WITH HIS SISTER.

THE WOUNDS OPEN ON HIS BODY LIKE RED FLOWERS. HE CAN'T EVEN SCREAM. THE FIRST SLASH CUTS HIS THROAT.

THIS MOMENT MEETS THAT ONE. WHAT MIGHT BE BECOMES WHAT IS.

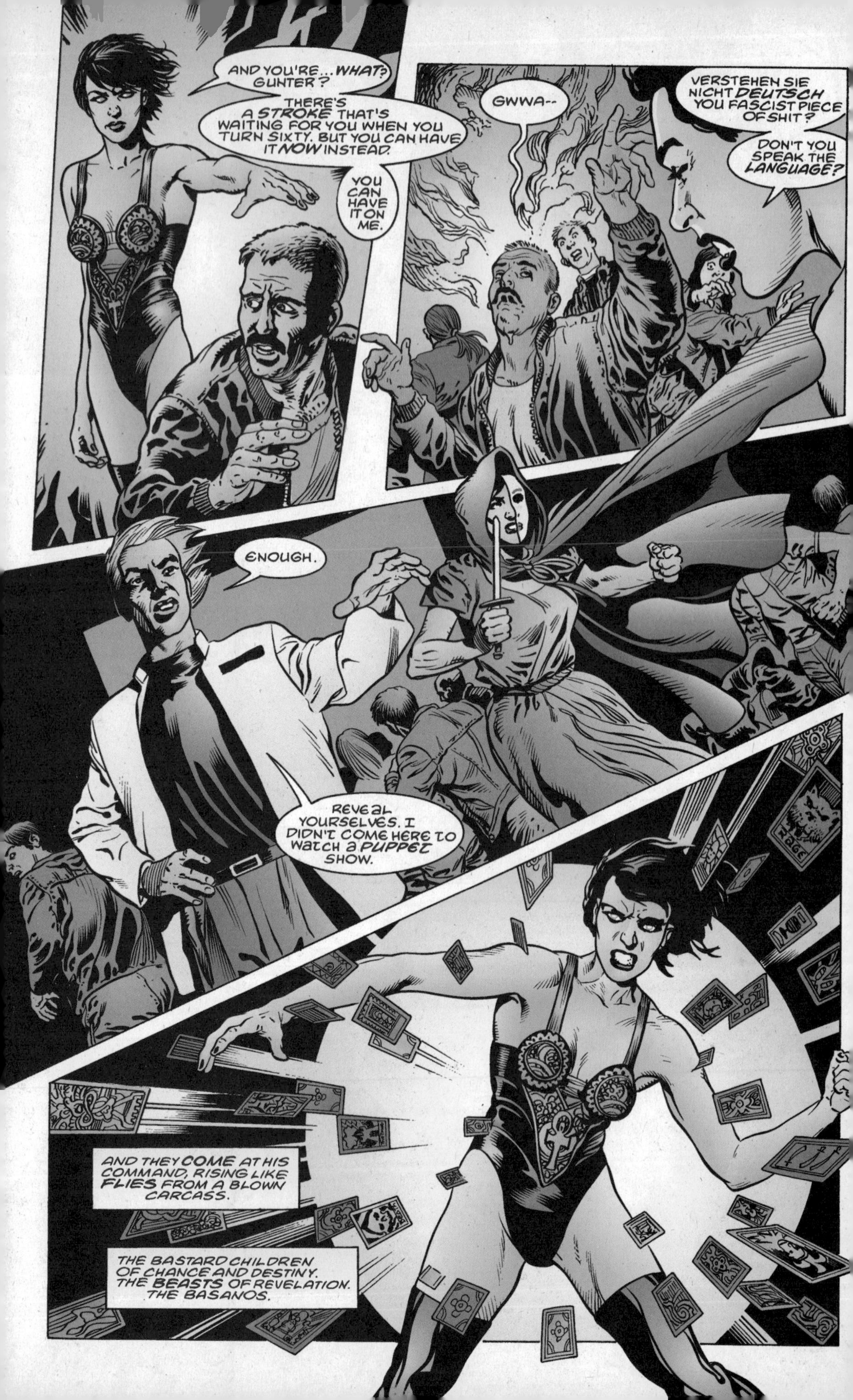
AND YOU'RE... WHAT? GUNTER?
THERE'S A STROKE THAT'S WAITING FOR YOU WHEN YOU TURN SIXTY. BUT YOU CAN HAVE IT NOW INSTEAD.
YOU CAN HAVE IT ON ME.
GWWA--
VERSTEHEN SIE NICHT DEUTSCH YOU FASCIST PIECE OF SHIT?
DON'T YOU SPEAK THE LANGUAGE?
ENOUGH.
REVEAL YOURSELVES. I DIDN'T COME HERE TO WATCH A PUPPET SHOW.
AND THEY COME AT HIS COMMAND, RISING LIKE FLIES FROM A BLOWN CARCASS.
THE BASTARD CHILDREN OF CHANCE AND DESTINY. THE BEASTS OF REVELATION. THE BASANOS.

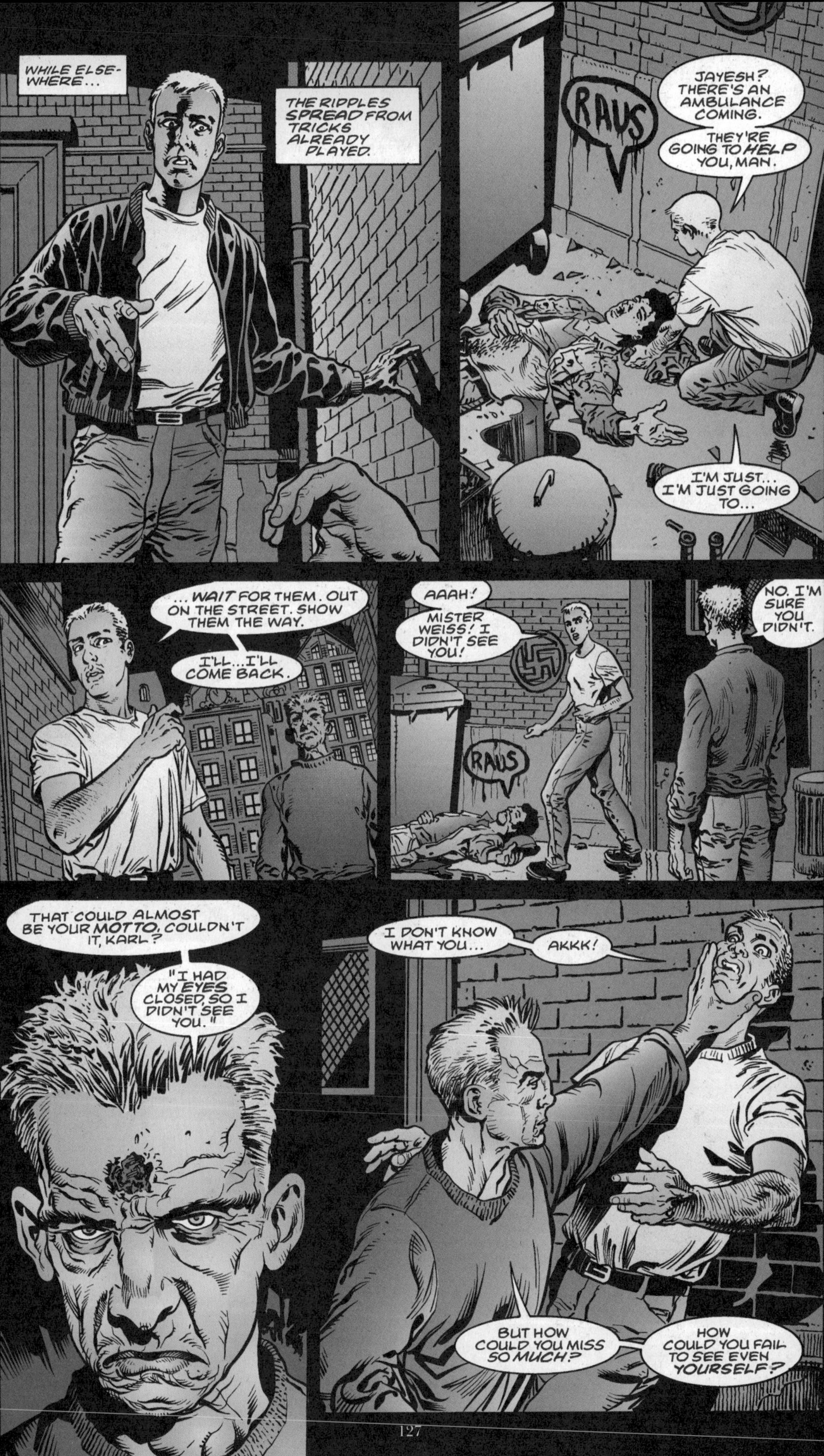
WHILE ELSE-WHERE...
THE RIPPLES SPREAD FROM TRICKS ALREADY PLAYED.
RAUS
JAYESH? THERE'S AN AMBULANCE COMING.
THEY'RE GOING TO HELP YOU, MAN.
I'M JUST... I'M JUST GOING TO...
...WAIT FOR THEM. OUT ON THE STREET. SHOW THEM THE WAY.
I'LL...I'LL COME BACK.
AAAH!
MISTER WEISS! I DIDN'T SEE YOU!
RAUS
NO. I'M SURE YOU DIDN'T.
THAT COULD ALMOST BE YOUR MOTTO, COULDN'T IT, KARL?
"I HAD MY EYES CLOSED, SO I DIDN'T SEE YOU."
I DON'T KNOW WHAT YOU...
AKKK!
BUT HOW COULD YOU MISS SO MUCH?
HOW COULD YOU FAIL TO SEE EVEN YOURSELF?

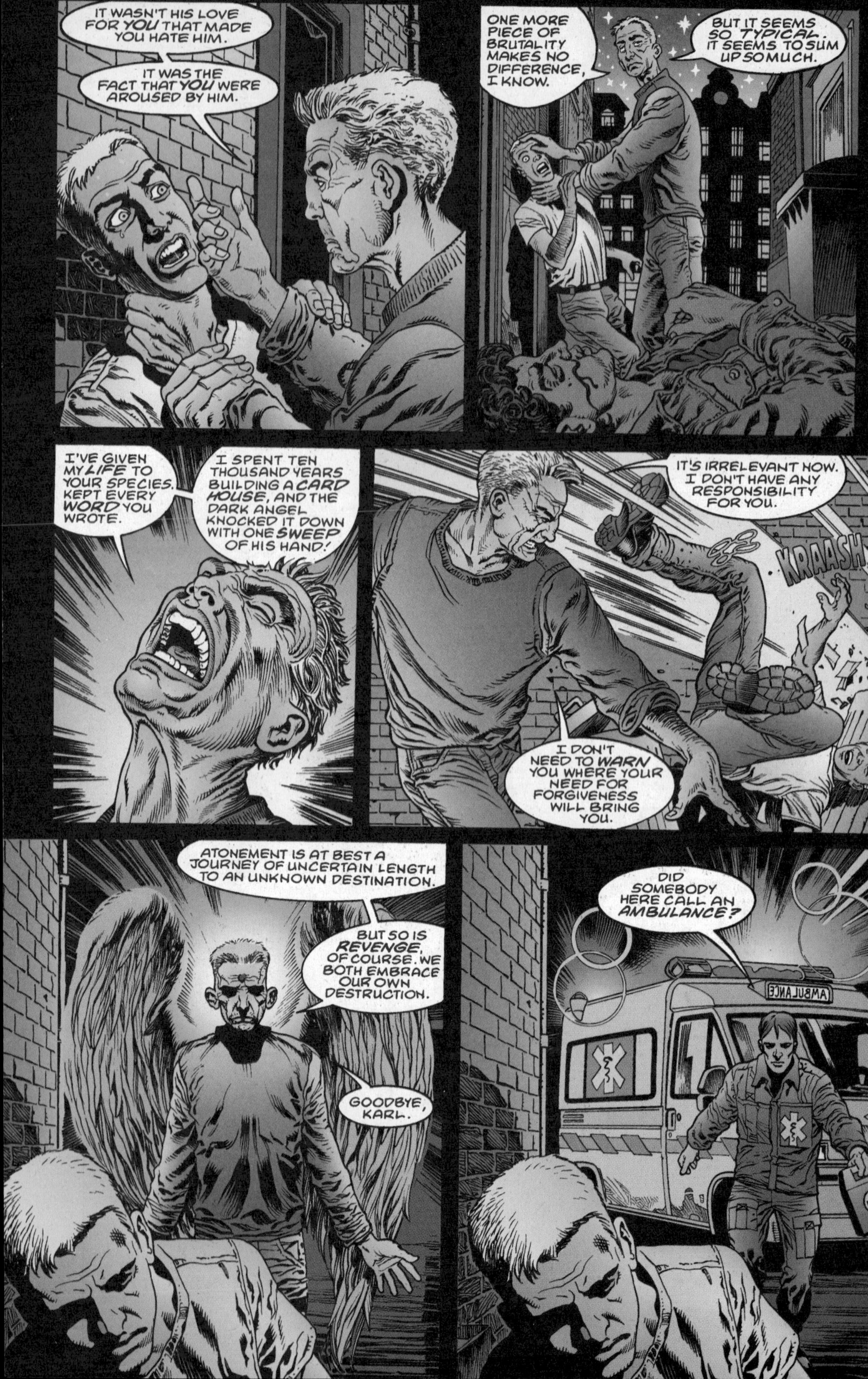
IT WASN'T HIS LOVE FOR YOU THAT MADE YOU HATE HIM.
IT WAS THE FACT THAT YOU WERE AROUSED BY HIM.
ONE MORE PIECE OF BRUTALITY MAKES NO DIFFERENCE, I KNOW.
BUT IT SEEMS SO TYPICAL. IT SEEMS TO SUM UP SO MUCH.
I'VE GIVEN MY LIFE TO YOUR SPECIES. KEPT EVERY WORD YOU WROTE.
I SPENT TEN THOUSAND YEARS BUILDING A CARD HOUSE, AND THE DARK ANGEL KNOCKED IT DOWN WITH ONE SWEEP OF HIS HAND!
IT'S IRRELEVANT NOW. I DON'T HAVE ANY RESPONSIBILITY FOR YOU.
KRAASH
I DON'T NEED TO WARN YOU WHERE YOUR NEED FOR FORGIVENESS WILL BRING YOU.
ATONEMENT IS AT BEST A JOURNEY OF UNCERTAIN LENGTH TO AN UNKNOWN DESTINATION.
BUT SO IS REVENGE, OF COURSE. WE BOTH EMBRACE OUR OWN DESTRUCTION.
GOODBYE, KARL.
DID SOMEBODY HERE CALL AN AMBULANCE?
AMBULANCE

THE CARDS SEEM TO KNOW THAT THEY CAN'T WIN BY DIRECT ATTACK. THESE ARE THE TACTICS OF DIVERSION.

FEINT AND WEAVE, STAB AND RETREAT.

FOR A MOMENT, AT LEAST, THEY SEEM TO WORK.

THAT ONE, MAZIKEEN.

NOW.

NOTHING HUMAN COULD MOVE SO FAST. THE CARDS RISE LIKE STARTLED BIRDS.

ALL BUT ONE.

SOMETHING TEARS INSIDE HER. SOFT MEMBRANES SLICED CLEAN THROUGH. COLD METAL SHEATHES ITSELF IN HER GUT.

SHE TRIES TO SCREAM.

BUT THERE'S NO AIR LEFT.

THE LIGHTBRINGER

129

LUCIFER. SUNLIGHTER. OATH-BREAKER.

GIVE US OUR BROTHER BACK OR YOU'LL *TWIST* ON THE AXLE TREE OF HEAVEN LIKE A GAME-COCK ON A *GIBBET!*

YOU *FORGET* YOUR-SELF.

I AM CONSIDERING WHETHER OR NOT TO *PARDON* YOU. IN THE MEANTIME, I REQUIRE A DIVINATION.

YOU WILL OBLIGE ME.

YOUR WILL BE *DONE,* DREAD LORD.

AS IT NO LONGER IS IN HELL OR HEAVEN.

I STAND AT A CROSS-ROADS. ILLUMINATE THE PATHS.

VERY WELL.

THIS... THIS *SHOWS* HIM.

THE LORD OF NO REALM. THE *APOSTATE.* PINNED ON A DILEMMA.

GOD HOLDS THE *DOOR* FOR YOU LIKE A FAWNING FOOTMAN, BUT WHERE DOES IT LEAD?

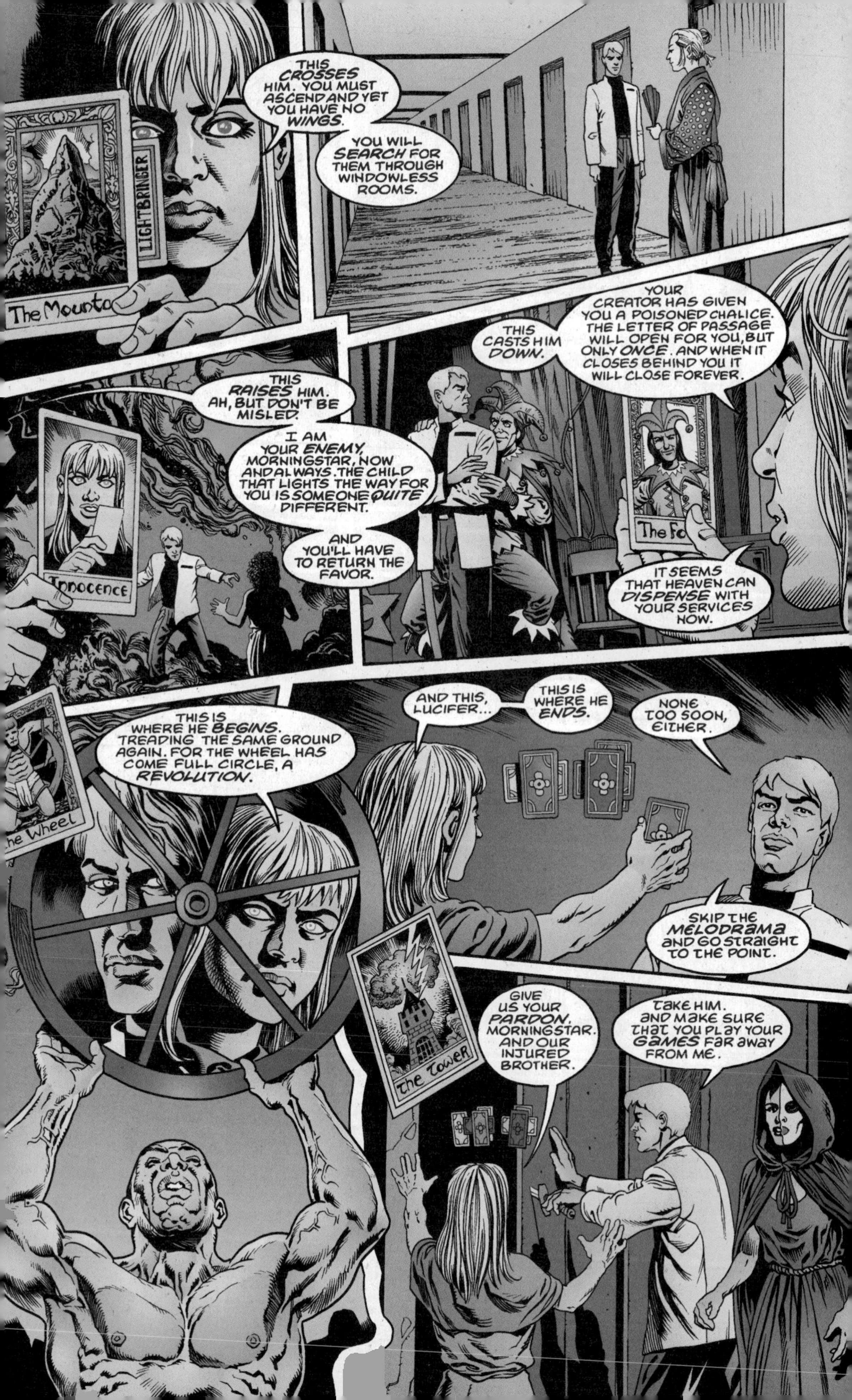

The Mounta
LIGHTBRINGER
THIS CROSSES HIM. YOU MUST ASCEND AND YET YOU HAVE NO WINGS.
YOU WILL SEARCH FOR THEM THROUGH WINDOWLESS ROOMS.
THIS CASTS HIM DOWN.
YOUR CREATOR HAS GIVEN YOU A POISONED CHALICE. THE LETTER OF PASSAGE WILL OPEN FOR YOU, BUT ONLY ONCE. AND WHEN IT CLOSES BEHIND YOU IT WILL CLOSE FOREVER.
The Fo
IT SEEMS THAT HEAVEN CAN DISPENSE WITH YOUR SERVICES NOW.
THIS RAISES HIM. AH, BUT DON'T BE MISLED.
I AM YOUR ENEMY, MORNINGSTAR, NOW AND ALWAYS. THE CHILD THAT LIGHTS THE WAY FOR YOU IS SOMEONE QUITE DIFFERENT.
AND YOU'LL HAVE TO RETURN THE FAVOR.
Innocence
he Wheel
THIS IS WHERE HE BEGINS. TREADING THE SAME GROUND AGAIN. FOR THE WHEEL HAS COME FULL CIRCLE, A REVOLUTION.
AND THIS, LUCIFER...
THIS IS WHERE HE ENDS.
NONE TOO SOON, EITHER.
SKIP THE MELODRAMA AND GO STRAIGHT TO THE POINT.
the Tower
GIVE US YOUR PARDON, MORNINGSTAR. AND OUR INJURED BROTHER.
TAKE HIM. AND MAKE SURE THAT YOU PLAY YOUR GAMES FAR AWAY FROM ME.

WE HAVE WHAT WE CAME FOR, MAZIKEEN, BUT KEEP THIS HANDY.

YESZH, RROAHD.

UUUUUH!

WELL THAT'S *THAT* THEN. CONSUMMATUM EST.

TIME FOR YOU TO *DECIDE*, JILL. YES OR NO?

Y...YES OR NO TO *WHAT?* I DON'T UNDERSTAND.

TO *US*. WE CAN ONLY STAY IF YOU ACCEPT US OF YOUR OWN FREE WILL. IT'S A BARGAIN.

A *CONTRACT*.

YOU'VE SEEN THE SMALLEST *GLIMPSE* OF WHAT WE CAN GIVE YOU.

SUCCESS AND FAME WILL COME TO YOU WITHOUT YOUR NEEDING TO *TRY*. OH, AND YOU'LL LIVE *FOREVER*, IF THAT'S ANY INCENTIVE.

SAY YES, DAUGHTER OF EVE. LET US LIVE IN YOU.

DEATH

AND WHAT CAN SHE SAY? THE *TASTE* IN HER MOUTH IS THE TASTE OF TWELVE WASTED YEARS. CLIMBING. FALLING.

LIKE HER FATHER, DANGLING ON A STRING.

THE *SOUND* SHE HEARS IS HER MOTHER'S VOICE, TELLING HER SHE'LL NEVER AMOUNT TO JACK SHIT.

AND SHE GETS THIS FEELING, LIKE ALL HER LIFE IS *STIGMATA*.

OLD WOUNDS THAT STAY MIRACULOUSLY OPEN.

132

HEY. MISTER DEVA.

EXCUSE ME.

YES?

HAS HE...HAS HE WOKEN UP YET?

THEY CANNOT SAY FOR SURE THAT HE *WILL* WAKE UP.

THERE IS BLEEDING IN THE *BRAIN*, YOU SEE.

THEY SAY IT IS A HARD THING TO *CURE*.

OUR SON WOULD BE DEAD ALREADY IF YOU HAD NOT FOUND HIM.

BLESS YOU FOR THAT. BLESS YOU.

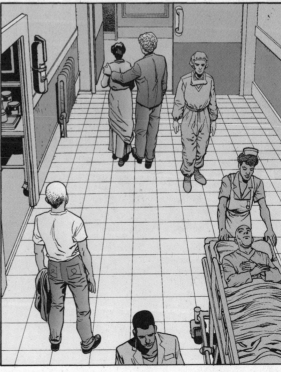

IF HIS BLOOD PRESSURE *FALLS* ANY FURTHER, PAGE ME. OTHERWISE I'LL SEE HIM ON WARD ROUNDS IN THE MORNING.

YES, DOCTOR.

SO ANYWAY.

HOW WAS *YOUR* DAY?

TWO OF THEM ARE *DEAD, JAY, AND ONE'S QUADRIPLEGIC.*

THE ONE OUTSIDE... WELL, *TRUST* ME WHEN I TELL YOU HE'LL GET HIS SOME *OTHER* WAY.

I DON'T THINK I COULD KILL HIM IN COLD BLOOD. WELL, MAYBE WITH MY COOKING...

I'LL COME BACK AND *SEE* YOU. I PROMISE.

IN THE MEANTIME, KEEP AN EYE OUT FOR ME.

"I'LL BE HARD TO MISS."

ALL DONE?

YOU'VE GOT ME *COLD,* HAVEN'T YOU?

YOU CAN SEE THE INSIDE OF MY *HEAD.* SO YOU KNEW WHICH WAY I'D JUMP ALL ALONG.

WE KNOW WHICH WAY *EVERY-ONE* JUMPS.

THOSE WHO BELIEVE IN FREE WILL MAKE THE BEST *PUPPETS* OF ALL.

134

A ONE-WAY TICKET. A DOOR THAT OPENS ONLY FROM *THIS* SIDE.

I DON'T KNOW IF I'M MORE OFFENDED BY THE *DECEIT* OR BY THE INSULT TO MY *INTELLIGENCE.*

I THOUGHT I'D PROVED MY POINT, BUT EVIDENTLY YOU'RE VERY *SLOW* ON THE UPTAKE.

YOU'VE GOT NO ONE TO *BLAME* FOR THIS BUT YOURSELF.

MAZIKEEN, GIVE ME THE KNIFE.

HE IS NO LONGER THE LORD OF HELL.

HE IS NO LONGER THE AGENT OF HEAVEN.

WHAT IS HE *NOW?* WHAT NAME DENOTES HIS FUNCTION?

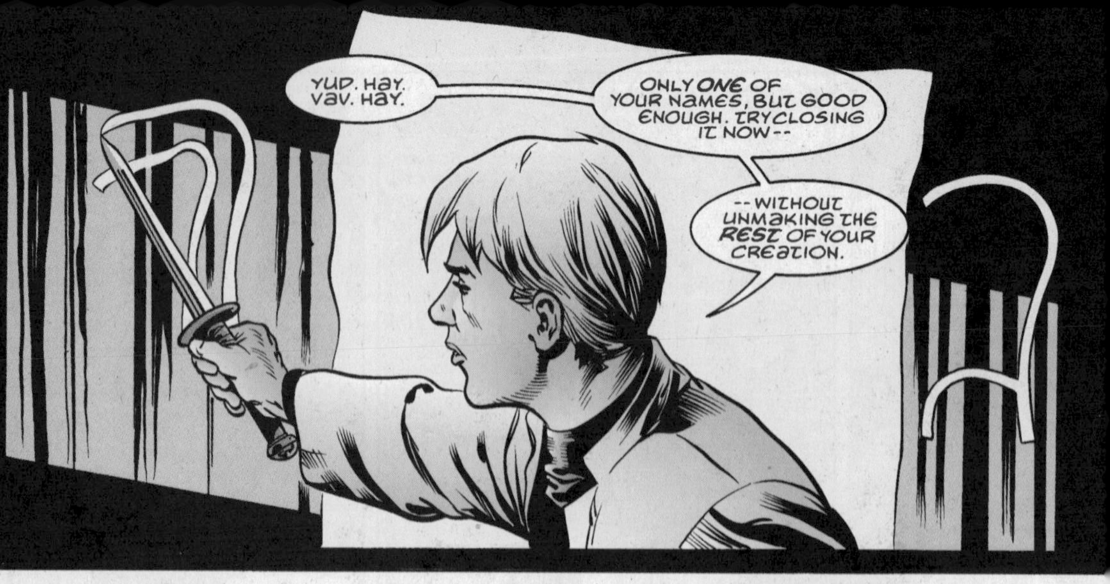
YUD. HAY. VAV. HAY.
ONLY ONE OF YOUR NAMES, BUT GOOD ENOUGH. TRY CLOSING IT NOW--
--WITHOUT UNMAKING THE REST OF YOUR CREATION.

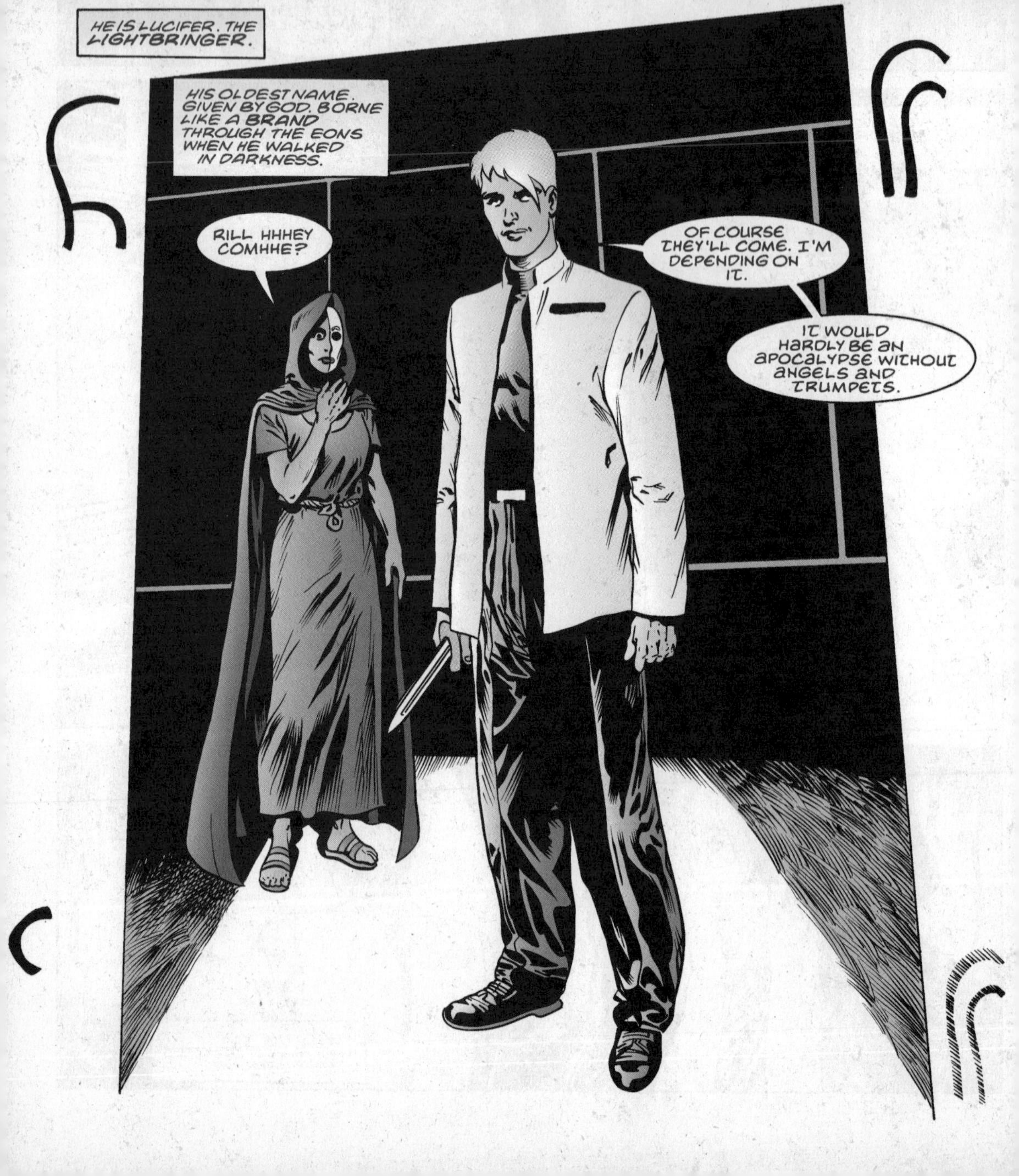
HE IS LUCIFER. THE LIGHTBRINGER.
HIS OLDEST NAME. GIVEN BY GOD. BORNE LIKE A BRAND THROUGH THE EONS WHEN HE WALKED IN DARKNESS.
RILL HHHEY COMHHE?
OF COURSE THEY'LL COME. I'M DEPENDING ON IT.
IT WOULD HARDLY BE AN APOCALYPSE WITHOUT ANGELS AND TRUMPETS.

Born with the DEAD

Tuesday, 15th November. Mona's funeral. I knew it was coming so I was okay with it. Sort of.

But I had to go straight from SCHOOL, and Dad didn't bring me a change of clothes.

And of course all the dead people were watching me from the other graves. It's really hard to pretend they're not there.

Mona's Mum was crying and her face was all red, but she wasn't THINKING about anything much.

Her Dad had the same creepy crawly things in his mind that he ALWAYS has. Money, and tied-up women, and all the different kinds of DRUGS he sells. Yeuk.

mike carey	warren pleece	dean ormston	daniel vozzo	ellie de ville	will dennis	shelly roeberg
writer	layouts	finishes	colorist & seps	letterer	assistant editor	editor

based on the character created by gaiman, kieth & dringenberg

I remember I went round to Mona's house after school. He never looked at us ONCE. He just talked on his phone the whole time, to lots of people.

NOT EVEN IN YOUR EAR? IT'S REALLY COOL. SCARY SPICE HAS GOT ONE IN HER TONGUE.

MY DAD WOULD GO CRAZY.

Until Mona put on IF YOU WANNA BE MY LOVER and we DANCED.

He kept on shouting for a long time, but only at MONA: it was like I wasn't even there.

The vicar said god loves children MOST of all. I mean CHILDREN! Mona was twelve. She had her PERIOD and everything.

I didn't listen to the rest of it. I was thinking why did she DO it?

Without even TELLING me something was wrong.

Then Mum went back to work and Dad drove me home.

And all the way he was feeling RELIEVED, like "thank god that's over and I can drop this sad face."

Only it WASN'T over. The worst part still hadn't happened yet.

And by this time I REALLY wanted to get it over with.

ELAINE. DON'T TURN ON THE LIGHT. PLEASE.

I LOOK A REAL MESS.

HELLO, MONA. WHAT TOOK YOU SO LONG?

WELL, IT WAS HARD TO THINK, AT FIRST. IT WAS THE NORTH CIRCULAR.

SEVEN OR EIGHT CARS WENT OVER ME BEFORE THEY COULD STOP.

THEN I WENT HOME, BUT NO ONE COULD SEE ME. SO I CAME TO YOU BECAUSE...BECAUSE YOU WERE SORT OF SHINING AND I COULD SEE YOU FROM A LONG WAY AWAY.

I'M SORRY. I'M LEAVING BLOOD ALL ON YOUR BED.

NO YOU'RE NOT. YOU'RE NOT REALLY BLEEDING. AND YOU DON'T HAVE TO LOOK LIKE THAT, EITHER.

I DON'T?

NO, IT'S JUST WHAT YOU...YOU KNOW, WHAT YOU'RE *EXPECTING* BECAUSE OF HOW YOU DIED. YOU CAN LOOK LIKE BRITTNEY SPEARS IF YOU WANT TO.

WHY'D YOU DO IT, MONA? WHY'D YOU GO AND WALK UNDER A *CAR*?

THAT'S GREAT! THAT'S *REALLY* GREAT! I KNEW YOU'D COME ON LIKE MY MUM!

DO YOU THINK I *WANTED* TO BE DEAD?

WELL *DIDN'T* YOU? I MEAN, I THOUGHT... YOU KNOW... IT WAS BECAUSE YOUR *DAD* WAS...

NO I *DIDN'T*, ELAINE BELLOC!

I WAS BLOODY *MURDERED*, IF YOU MUST KNOW!

MURDERED?

MONA, DON'T *SAY* THINGS LIKE THAT!

IT'S TRUE. SOME M...MAN JUST CAME UP BEHIND ME AND THREW ME OFF THE OVERPASS. RIGHT INTO THE TRAFFIC.

OH MY GOD. THEN I... I'VE GOT TO TELL SOMEONE. THIS WAS WHEN YOU WERE COMING OUT OF SCHOOL, RIGHT? DID ANYONE ELSE SEE?

NO. I HAD DETENTION. MR. WADDINGTON GAVE ME A WHOLE *HOUR* FOR RUNNING IN THE CORRIDORS.

THERE WAS NO ONE AROUND.

I DON'T EVEN KNOW WHY HE *DID* IT. HE JUST PICKED ME UP AND TH...THREW ME.

OH, I'M SO SCARED, I'M SO SCARED.

PLEASE, ELAINE. PLEASE HELP ME.

And that did it, I guess. At Northcote she was so much TOUGHER than me. She hit Gordon Bosch in the face once because he pushed me.

She never, NEVER cried.

COME ON, MONA. DON'T... DON'T GET UPSET, OKAY?

Then I remembered what Grandma Furness said -- about why some dead people lie DOWN and some don't.

WHAT ARE YOU DOING?

And I thought maybe there IS something I can do to help.

MONA, YOU'RE A TROUBLED SPIRIT. YOU'VE GOT UNFINISHED BUSINESS AND YOU WON'T BE ABLE TO LIE QUIET IN YOUR GRAVE UNTIL IT'S ALL SORTED.

COME OVER HERE.

Most of them just come when I say their NAMES, but Grandma Furness said I should light a candle or a torch.

"Just for the sake of RESPECT."

GRANDMA DICKMAN, GRANDMA SHAW, GRANDMA FURNESS.

CAN YOU COME, PLEASE? I KNOW IT'S STILL DAY-LIGHT BUT IT'S REALLY, REALLY IMPORTANT.

WH...WHAT'S HAPPENING? STOP IT, ELAINE!

THEY'RE JUST GHOSTS, MONA. YOU CAN'T BE SCARED OF GHOSTS.

Uhhhhh...

ANYWAY, THEY'RE ON *OUR* SIDE. IT'S THE GUY WHO KILLED YOU WHO'S GOT TO WORRY.

HELLO, DARLING.

HELLO, LAINIE. WHERE'S THE FIRE?

WHAT ARE YOU GETTING THESE OLD BIDDIES UP SO EARLY FOR?

GRANDMAS, THIS IS MY FRIEND, MONA. SHE...SHE WAS MURDERED.

AND SHE NEEDS A GUIDE TO THE DRY LANDS?

NO. SHE NEEDS REVENGE.

Grandma Furness used to be a WITCH. I knew she'd have some good ideas.

BLACK MAGIC. HEX THE BUGGER TILL 'E *BLEEDS* OUT OF 'IS EARS.

OH LORD, PEGGY, THAT'S NOT A THING FOR...

YOU CAN DO A *SUMMONING*. A LESSER DEMON WILL TELL YOU THE KILLER'S NAME.

AND THEN YOU CAN USE THE NAME TO *CURSE* 'IM.

BUT WE DON'T KNOW *HOW* TO SUMMON A DEMON, GRANDMA.

NOT EVEN A LESSER ONE.

SPILL *BLOOD*, MY POPPET, AND THEN DRINK IT. DANCE *NAKED*. CALL HIS NAME.

IF HE'S *MINDED* TO COME HE WON'T BE HOLDING OFF FOR SPELLS OR CANDLES.

Great. Where was I going to get fresh BLOOD in Kensal Rise?

I came up with some pretty gross ideas, but in the end I just borrowed some from the kitchen.

Wussy or what?

Then I did a sort of stupid DISCO dance. I kept my underwear on because I didn't want a demon to see me naked.

I shouted three names. Grandma Furness said they were all good.

NOTHING'S HAPPENING, ELAINE.

I DON'T THINK THIS IS GOING TO WORK.

What I did next was pretty stupid. But I felt like such a PRAT standing there in my underwear.

HELLO, SATAN! HELLO, LUCIFER! ARE YOU RECEIVING ME?

ARE YOU MAZED, GIRL? BE SILENT!

IF HE DEIGNED TO ANSWER YOU, HE'D SHRIVEL YOUR SOUL LIKE A SALTED SLUG!

YOU KNOW WE COULD DO NOTHING BUT WATCH!

I'M SORRY.

IT WAS WRONG TO MAKE HER TRY, PEGGY FURNESS.

A CHILD DOING BLACK MAGIC!

AYE, WELL THAT'S THE NUB OF IT, I SUPPOSE.

YOU'RE TOO YOUNG, POPPET.

WHY SHOULD A DEMON HALE HIMSELF FROM THE HOBS OF HELL TO ANSWER A SPOTLESS VIRGIN WHO COULDN'T GIVE HER SOUL AWAY IF SHE TRIED?

THERE'S NO PROFIT IN IT.

That was when Dad called me down for supper.

IT'S OKAY, MONA. THERE'S SOMETHING ELSE WE CAN TRY TOMORROW.

DON'T WORRY. WE'LL GET HIM.

It's a good job I've got the grandmas.

Mum just talks about shares and investments and stuff and Dad's only into his book reviews

They wouldn't know the first THING about finding a murderer.

The next morning we set off for school. When we got to the end of the road I turned LEFT instead of right. To the Roundhey estate. To Mona's school.

But when we got close to the North Circular we could hear the cars. Mona got really scared.

IS THIS WHERE IT HAPPENED?

OVER THERE. BY THE POSTERS.

I'LL STAY HERE, ELAINE. IS IT OKAY IF I STAY HERE?

Looking into the past is sort of like whole-school ASSEMBLY. Where you sit on the balcony and you're looking down and there are so many faces you can't really see any of them.

Because the past doesn't STOP. The more you look, the more of it there is.

I thought I could see Mona. And maybe there WAS a man — near her, moving around her, before she fell --

-- But moving too fast, in the dark, and her fear was still fresh, like a big STAIN over everything. I couldn't see his face.

So I kept on looking backwards — further away in time. Keeping my EYES on him as he went back and back, always the same distance behind Mona.

Across the overpass and back down the Sutton Road. To the gates...

He was FOLLOWING her.

ROUNDHEY COMPREHENSIVE

LONDON BOROUGH OF BRENT

All the way from the school.

WHERE DID YOU DO YOUR DETENTION?

B-12. IT'S THAT WAY. ELAINE...

...HOW COME YOU CAN SEE ME WHEN MY MUM AND DAD COULDN'T?

IT'S NOT JUST DEAD PEOPLE. REMEMBER IN YEAR THREE WHEN MRS. SEWELL GOT CANCER?

YOU COULD SEE THAT?

I COULD HEAR IT. B-12, RIGHT?

It was just a ROOM. A school room. Horrible old wood polish smell. Crummy old desks with the chairs fixed in.

At Bishop Laud we have CARPETS. And chairs with legs.

HE WASN'T WITH YOU IN HERE. HE MUST'VE--

EXCUSE ME! YOU, GIRL! WHAT ARE YOU DOING OUT OF CLASS?

OH NO! ELAINE, IT'S MR. WADDINGTON! MY HEADMASTER!

THAT ISN'T A ROUNDHEY UNIFORM. WHO ARE YOU?

I'M SORRY, SIR. I CAME TO... TO TELL MY FRIEND SOMETHING. SHE'S IN...

...IN MONA DOYLE'S CLASS.

145

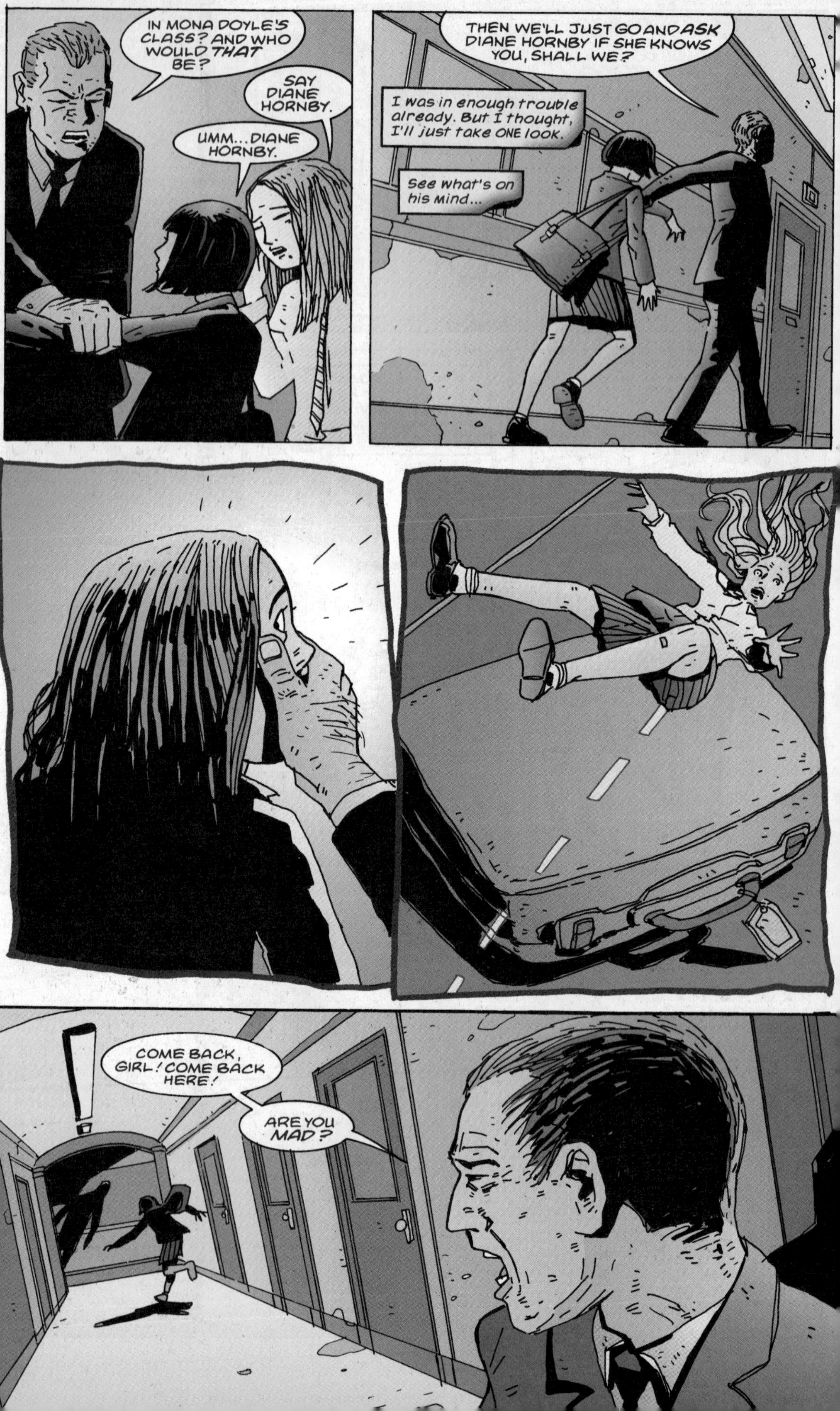
IN MONA DOYLE'S CLASS? AND WHO WOULD *THAT* BE?
SAY DIANE HORNBY.
UMM... DIANE HORNBY.
THEN WE'LL JUST GO AND *ASK* DIANE HORNBY IF SHE KNOWS YOU, SHALL WE?
I was in enough trouble already. But I thought, I'll just take ONE look.
See what's on his mind...
COME BACK, GIRL! COME BACK HERE!
ARE YOU *MAD*?

I CAN'T TELL YOU HOW *SORRY* WE ARE. THEY WERE BEST FRIENDS ALL THROUGH PRIMARY SCHOOL...

NO, NO, MR. BELLOC. NO HARM DONE.

IT'S VERY *HARD* FOR CHILDREN TO COPE WITH SUCH A SUDDEN LOSS -- HARD FOR ALL OF US.

YOUNG GIRLS GET VERY INVOLVED IN THESE ROMANTIC FRIENDSHIPS. SHARE THEIR... *SECRETS*, AND SO ON.

BUT TIME IS A GREAT HEALER.

I JUST WISH YOU'D *TALKED* TO US, ELAINE.

I'M SORRY, DAD. I WANTED TO SEE... WHERE SHE DIED. *PLEASE* DON'T GET MAD.

I'M NOT MAD. I'M DISAPPOINTED.

DODO ICE GIRLS

I got the Dad treatment, then the Mum treatment, but not the Mona treatment. She didn't come back that night.

She always hated getting into trouble. Maybe she just wanted to forget the whole thing now. Get on with being dead.

But I didn't. Things look *DIFFERENT* when you've been inside a murderer.

And if Mona didn't know how to be an unquiet spirit, I'd just have to do it *MYSELF*.

I waited until about one -- nothing but snores from Mum and Dad's room. Mr. Waddington lived in Burnt Oak. I fished that out of his SECRETARY'S thoughts.

There was a night bus that would take me to Brent Cross, and then I could walk it.

All the way there I kept seeing that stuff that was in his mind. He was thinking about killing Mona.

But he was thinking about this suitcase, too. In his garage. As though Mona REMINDED him of it.

So I thought, if I get a look inside the case there might be some kind of PROOF that he did it.

Halfway along Burnt Oak Broadway, I felt this kind of prickling. Like someone was BREATHING on my neck.

ELAINE, I'M SORRY I RAN AWAY. I WOULD'VE COME BACK BEFORE, BUT...

...THERE'S THIS GIRL WHO'S FOLLOWING ME AROUND. I'VE BEEN TRYING TO LOSE HER.

BLACK HAIR AND AMAZING EYE SHADOW, RIGHT? YOU CAN'T LOSE HER, MONA.

BUT YOU'RE OKAY IF WE STICK TOGETHER. ANYONE WHO'S WITH ME, SHE SORT OF IGNORES.

YOU SAY "TILL DEATH US DO PART" -- YOU KNOW, LIKE IN A WEDDING. IT MEANS YOU'LL KEEP THE SECRET FOR- EVER.

TILL DEATH US DO PART.

It felt GOOD having Mona there. It made me think about when I was nine and we used to do everything together.

About dancing to THE SPICE GIRLS singing that friendship never ends.

Like THEY know.

Dad used to work for the RAC, and he had a set of keys that he used to open cars when people locked themselves out.

Some of the keys were called SKELETONS, and he told me once they worked on any lock.

CLICK

It didn't take long at all.

MONA?

ARE THESE WHAT I THINK THEY ARE?

THEY'RE DRUGS—LIKE MY DAD SELLS. THAT ONE'S SPEED, AND THE LITTLE SACHETS ARE KETAMINE AND THE STUFF IN THE BOTTLES IS CALLED POPPERS.

THEN WHAT'S YOUR *HEADMASTER* DOING WITH THEM?

DO YOU THINK HE WAS *BUYING* THEM FROM YOUR DAD? COULD HE HAVE KILLED YOU BECAUSE... BECAUSE YOUR DAD OWED HIM *MONEY* OR SOMETHING?

MAYBE. BUT THERE'S A *LOT* THERE. MOST PEOPLE WOULD JUST BUY ONE OR TWO HITS AT A TIME.

WELL, IT DOESN'T MATTER ANYWAY. I'M TAKING SOME OF EVERYTHING.

WE CAN SEND THIS STUFF TO THE POLICE.

I BET HE'LL LOSE HIS *JOB*, AT LEA...

LOSE MY JOB? LOSE MY *JOB*?

THAT'S *NOTHING* COMPARED TO WHAT YOU'RE GOING TO LOSE, GIRL!

It was feeling so scared that woke me up. I was choking on it. I couldn't even THINK except to think afraid, afraid, afraid.

I wanted to run...

And I couldn't move.

I CARE ABOUT MY WORK, YOU KNOW?

I'VE MADE SOME BAD DECISIONS, BUT I REALLY DO CARE. ABOUT THE SCHOOL-- THE KIDS.

IF YOU WEIGH UP THE GOOD AND THE HARM I'VE DONE, ANYONE WOULD SAY I'M A DECENT MAN.

SO... WHO ELSE KNOWS?

I tried to figure that out but I couldn't make my mind work. I was going to scream any second.

But part of me was standing off to one side, LOOKING at the fear...

And then the penny dropped. Most of it wasn't MINE. It was his.

So I took the thing that he was most afraid of right out of his mind, and I threw it back to him.

SHE KEPT A DIARY.

SHIT! *I* KNEW IT! WHERE DID YOU FIND IT? WHERE IS IT *NOW*?

AT...AT THE SCHOOL. ROOM B-12.

IT'S BEHIND THE *RADIATOR*.

WE'LL TAKE UP THIS CONVERSATION WHEN I GET BACK. IF YOU'RE *LYING* YOU'LL HAVE THE OCCASION TO BE VERY SORRY.

BUT YOU'RE... YOU'RE GOING TO KILL ME ANY-WAY.

TRUE. BUT I'VE GOT A GREAT DEAL OF DISCRETION ABOUT HOW *LONG* IT TAKES.

I heard the door slam and the car start. Then everything went QUIET again.

The school was only about three miles away. I didn't have long.

MONA?

HE'S GOING TO KILL *YOU* TOO! CALL YOUR GRANDMAS, ELAINE. THEY CAN DO MAGIC ON HIM!

NO THEY CAN'T. THEY'RE JUST GHOSTS.

THEY CAN'T DO ANYTHING ANY-MORE EXCEPT *TALK*.

SO LET'S TALK, MONA. THE WAY WE *USED* TO. LET'S SHARE SECRETS.

TELL ME ABOUT YOUR *DAD*.

IT WASN'T THERE.

S...SOMEONE MUST'VE *MOVED* IT. THAT'S WHERE IT WAS. *REALLY.*

PERHAPS. OR PERHAPS YOU *INVENTED* THE DIARY SO I'D LET YOU LIVE A LITTLE LONGER.

IN WHICH CASE I HOPE YOU GOT THE MOST YOU *COULD* OUT OF THE LAST TWENTY MINUTES.

I DID.

WHAT HAVE YOU *DONE* TO ME? WHAT DID YOU *DO?*

I... I BIT THEM OPEN AND THEN I DRIBBLED THEM INTO YOUR GLASS.

MR. WADDINGTON. I THINK...

...I THINK YOU'RE GOING TO *DIE.*

KETAMINE. IT'S *KETAMINE.* YOU'VE POISONED ME.

BITCH! BITCH! BITCH! I'LL *KILL* YOU.

OH GOD! OH GOD!

UUUHF!

He ran out into the hall. But Mona said, with a ketamine overdose there's not much POINT calling a doctor.

You've got to make yourself throw up really quick before your LUNGS stop working.

He was trying to dial. He was saying "Ambulance! Ambulance!" over and over again.

But everything was looking really strange now-- like looking through a MARBLE. It felt like there was this big chunk of ice inside my chest.

And I thought, this isn't fair. It's HIS death, not mine.

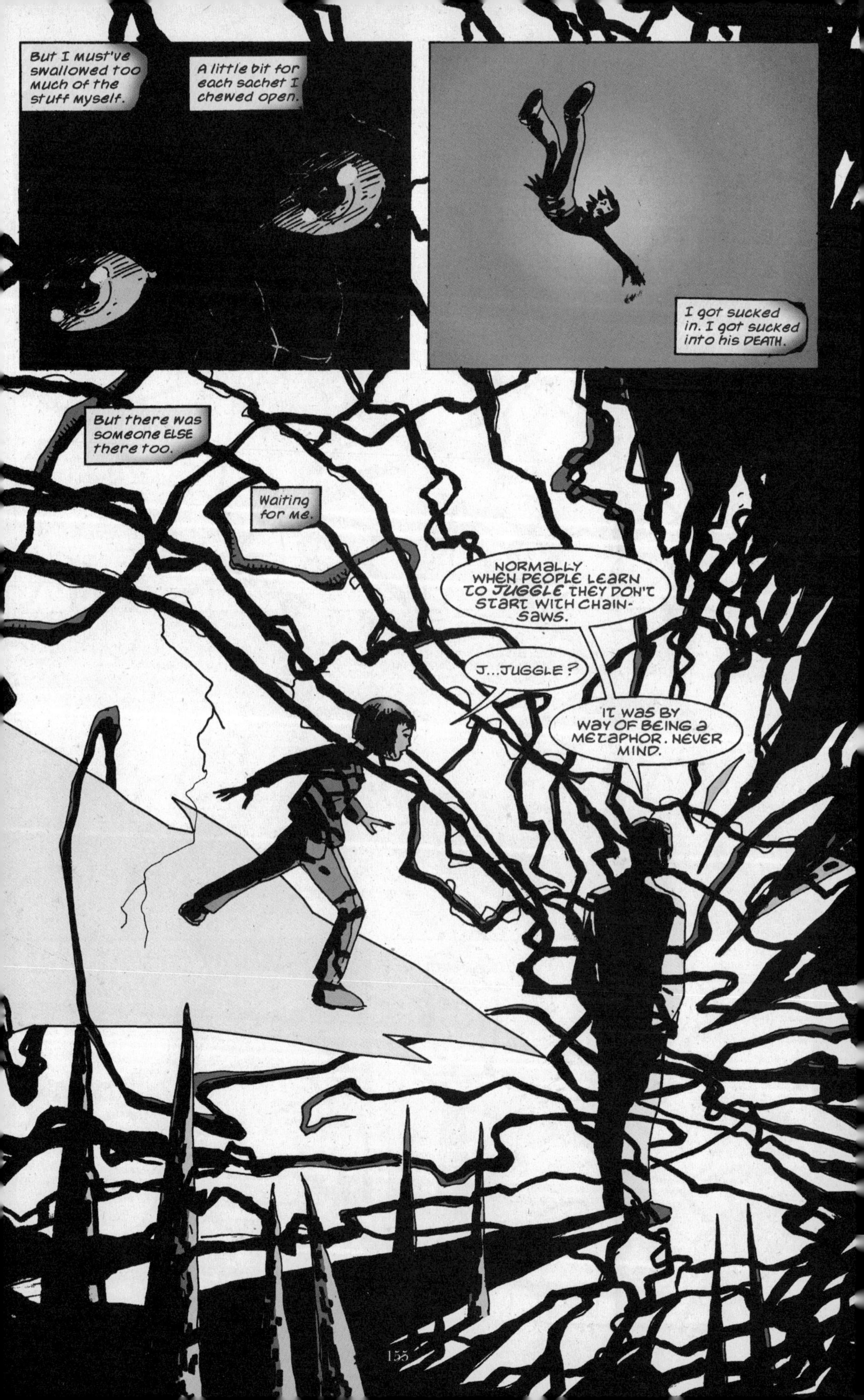
But I must've swallowed too much of the stuff myself.
A little bit for each sachet I chewed open.
I got sucked in. I got sucked into his DEATH.
But there was someone ELSE there too.
Waiting for me.
NORMALLY WHEN PEOPLE LEARN TO JUGGLE THEY DON'T START WITH CHAIN-SAWS.
J...JUGGLE?
IT WAS BY WAY OF BEING A METAPHOR. NEVER MIND.

WHERE ARE WE?

HMM?

OH, YOU'RE INSIDE HIS *MIND*. THE TEACHER'S. THE MAN YOU'RE IN THE PROCESS OF *MURDERING*.

OXYGEN STARVATION SQUEEZES THE DRUG HIGH INTO SYNAESTHETIC SCREAMS. IT *FEELS* EVEN WORSE THAN IT LOOKS.

It just sort of came to me then. Even though he didn't have any HORNS or anything.

YOU'RE... YOU'RE HIM. THE *DEVIL*.

I *SUMMONED* THE *DEVIL*.

DON'T *FLATTER* YOURSELF, CHILD. I'M NOT HERE BECAUSE YOU *CALLED* ME.

BUT I DID HEAR YOUR VOICE, AND I WANTED TO SEE FOR MYSELF.

SOMEONE HAS BEEN WORKING FOR A *VERY* LONG TIME. CHANCE ALONE COULDN'T ACCOUNT FOR YOU.

WILL HE DIE SOON? MR. WADDINGTON, I MEAN?

HE SHOULD BE DEAD *NOW*. I'M THE ONE WHO'S HOLDING HIM *BACK* FROM THAT MERCIFUL RELEASE.

BECAUSE AS THINGS STAND, HE'LL TAKE *YOU* WITH HIM. A DECK OF CARDS I MET RECENTLY SUGGESTED THAT I SHOULD KEEP YOU ALIVE.

NOW TAKE WHAT YOU WANT AND BE QUICK ABOUT IT. I HAVE OTHER ENGAGEMENTS.

YOU? BUT *WHY*?

I guess I knew what he meant. So I found it, Mona, and I took it. The TRUTH. About why Mr. Waddington KILLED you.

And even though the devil was in a hurry, I took a LONG time doing it. As long as I could.

That was our REVENGE, you see. That was how we got our own back on him.

It was stupid, really. HE was the one who was selling the drugs to your Dad.

Even went round to your flat a few years back.

He noticed you because you were reading MORE and Roundhey had just banned it.

MORE

When you started in year seven he RECOGNIZED you-- and he thought you recognized him, too. THAT'S why he killed you. To stop you from telling anyone.

And the crazy thing is, you DIDN'T remember him at all. He had nothing to be afraid of.

Until he met ME.

SATISFIED?

NO.

PITY. IT MAKES NO DIFFERENCE TO THE PRICE.

WH... WHERE ARE WE GOING?

WE? I AM GOING ON INTO THE REALMS OF PAIN.

YOU TO YOUR MORTAL BODY. BUT DON'T WORRY. I ALWAYS CALL IN WHAT'S OWED TO ME.

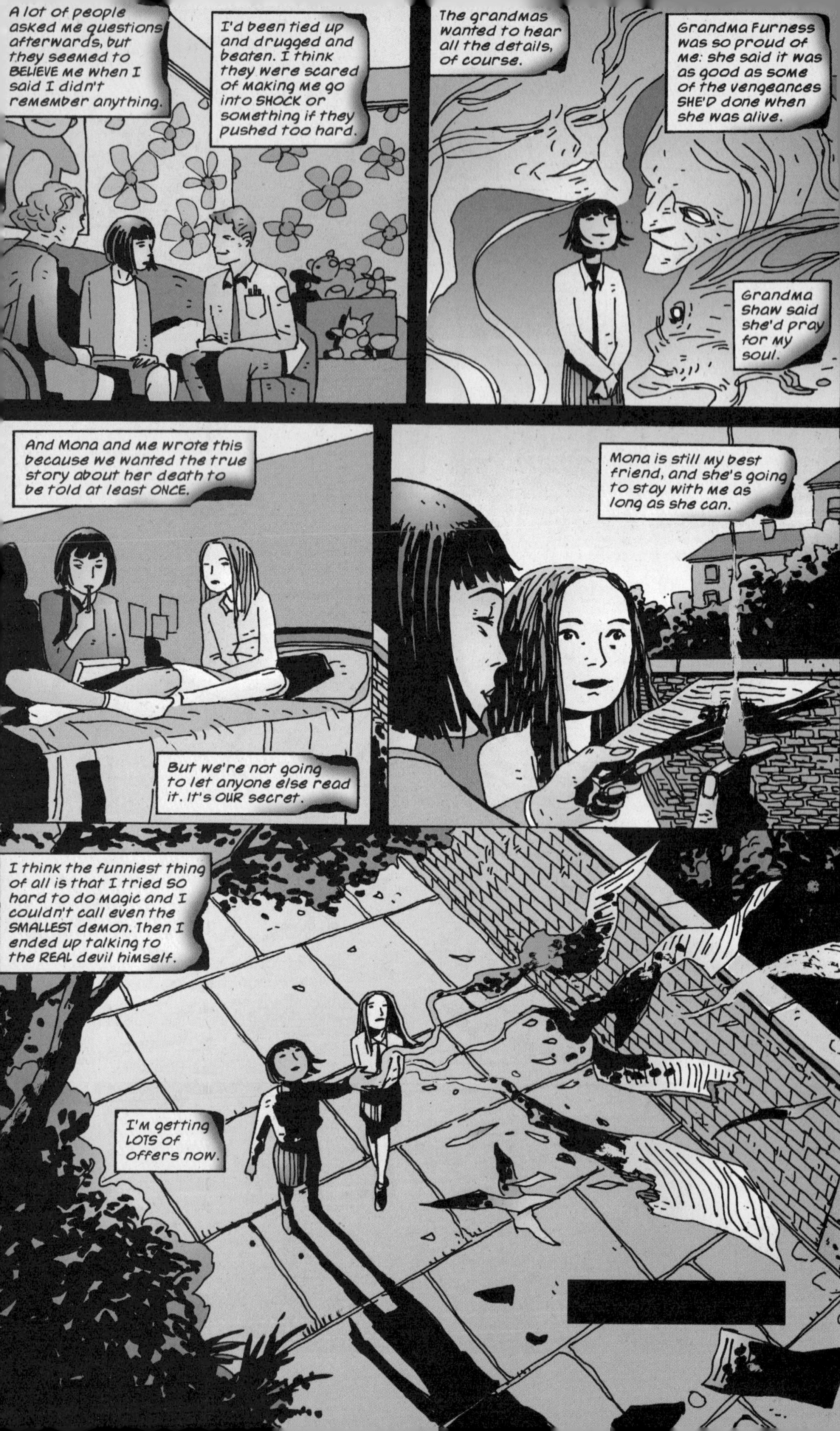
A lot of people asked me questions afterwards, but they seemed to BELIEVE me when I said I didn't remember anything.
I'd been tied up and drugged and beaten. I think they were scared of making me go into SHOCK or something if they pushed too hard.
The grandmas wanted to hear all the details, of course.
Grandma Furness was so proud of me: she said it was as good as some of the vengeances SHE'D done when she was alive.
Grandma Shaw said she'd pray for my soul.
And Mona and me wrote this because we wanted the true story about her death to be told at least ONCE.
But we're not going to let anyone else read it. It's OUR secret.
Mona is still my best friend, and she's going to stay with me as long as she can.
I think the funniest thing of all is that I tried SO hard to do magic and I couldn't call even the SMALLEST demon. Then I ended up talking to the REAL devil himself.
I'm getting LOTS of offers now.
[redacted]

THE LUCIFER LIBRARY

BOOK ONE: DEVIL IN THE GATEWAY

BOOK TWO: CHILDREN AND MONSTERS

BOOK THREE: A DALLIANCE WITH THE DAMNED

BOOK FOUR: THE DIVINE COMEDY

BOOK FIVE: INFERNO